Workshop on Human-Informed Translation and Interpreting Technology 2017

Held at RANLP 2017

Varna, Bulgaria
7 September 2017

ISBN: 978-1-5108-5547-2

Printed from e-media with permission by:

Curran Associates, Inc.
57 Morehouse Lane
Red Hook, NY 12571

Some format issues inherent in the e-media version may also appear in this print version.

Printed by Curran Associates, Inc. (2018)

For permission requests, please contact the Association for Computational Linguistics at the address below.

Association for Computational Linguistics
209 N. Eighth Street
Stroudsburg, Pennsylvania 18360

Phone: 1-570-476-8006
Fax: 1-570-476-0860

acl@aclweb.org

Additional copies of this publication are available from:

Curran Associates, Inc.
57 Morehouse Lane
Red Hook, NY 12571 USA
Phone: 845-758-0400
Fax: 845-758-2633
Email: curran@proceedings.com
Web: www.proceedings.com

RANLP 2017

The First Workshop on Human-Informed Translation and Interpreting Technology (HiT-IT)

Proceedings of the Workshop

September 7th, 2017
Varna, Bulgaria

Proceedings of the Workshop
Human-Informed Translation and Interpreting Technology
associated with RANLP 2017

Varna, Bulgaria
7 September 2017

Designed and Printed by INCOMA Ltd.
Shoumen, BULGARIA

Introduction

Human Translation and Machine Translation (MT) aim to solve the same problem (i.e. translating from one language into another) in two seemingly different ways.

There are many Natural Language Processing (NLP)/Computational linguistics efforts towards improving the work of translators and interpreters (for example Computer-Assisted Translation (CAT) tools, electronic dictionaries, concordancers, spell-checkers, terminological databases and terminology extraction tools, translation memories, partial machine translation of template documents, speech recognition systems for automatic subtitling, etc.). In turn, the NLP field makes use of the work and the knowledge of professional translators and interpreters to build models for automatic translation - e.g. by using parallel aligned text and speech corpora for text and speech machine translation learning, human evaluators of machine translation output, human annotations for automatic MT post-editing or using eye-tracking for learning editing patterns of professional translators, etc.

While there have been many workshops and conferences representing both sides: 1) Machine Translation in NLP (e.g. WMT, EAMT conferences), and 2) Automatic tools for translators and interpreters in Translation/Interpreting studies (e.g. Translating and The Computer, and the MT Summit conferences), there has not been a common publication & discussion venue for both sides. What makes our workshop unique is that it is a unified workshop which welcomes the contributions of both fields towards each other.

This workshop addresses BOTH the most recent developments in contributions of NLP to translation/interpreting and the contributions of translation/interpreting to NLP/MT. In this way it addresses the interests of researchers & specialists in both areas and their joint collaborations, aiming for example to improve their own tasks with the techniques & knowledge of the other field or to help the development of the other field with their own techniques & knowledge.

This year, we have received 11 high quality submissions, among which 8 have been accepted. Two articles have been accepted as full papers, and the rest six as short papers. Each submission has been reviewed by at least 2 reviewers, who were highly specialized experts either in human contributions to Machine Translation, or in Interpreting and Translation technologies, both from the computer science and Translation/Interpreting studies fields. The papers covered a broad spectrum of topics, such as:

- Automatic text simplification for translators
- Arabic dialects corpora creation for translators, interpreters and machine translation
- Extracting interpreting strategies, in order to improve speech-to-text machine translation
- Comparing machine translation and human translation
- NLP approaches & systems for building educational tools & resources for interpreters
- NLP approaches & systems for building educational tools & resources for translators
- Computer-assisted translation tools, such as translation memories, machine translation, etc.
- Translation resources, such as corpora, terminological databases, dictionaries
- Computer-assisted interpreting software, such as interpreters workbench, etc.
- Interpreting resources, such as corpora, terminological databases, dictionaries

- User requirements for interpreting and translation tools
- Methodologies for collecting user requirements
- Human accuracy metrics and human evaluation of machine translation
- Theoretical papers with translators/interpreters views on how machine translation should work/what output should produce
- Pre-editing and post-editing of machine translation
- Theoretical papers and practical applications on applying translation techniques & knowledge to NLP and machine translation
- Theoretical papers and practical applications on applying interpreting techniques & knowledge to NLP and machine translation

Our authors' nationalities & affiliations covered a wide range of countries, including: United Kingdom, Austria, Spain, Bulgaria, Jordan, Egypt, Qatar, Italy, Germany, Morocco, and United States.

The workshop also featured two invited talks on the topics of "The translation world and beyond... What's next? Don't get me wrong...", by Prof. Dr. Ruslan Mitkov, Director of the Research Institute in Information and Language Processing at the University of Wolverhampton, UK, and "Why are Computers (Still) Bad Translators?", provided by Dr. Preslav Nakov, Senior Scientist at the Qatar Computing Research Institute, HBKU. The workshop concluded with a vibrant round-table discussion.

We would like to thank the authors for submitting their articles to the HiT-IT Workshop, the members of the Programme Committee for their efforts to provide exhaustive reviews, even if the workshop was highly interdisciplinary, and the conference RANLP 2017, which has accepted us as a workshop and hosted us. We hope that all the participants received valuable feedback about their research as well as found their place in the fuzzy interdisciplinary field between human and machine translation.

Irina Temnikova, Constantin Orăsan, Gloria Corpas and Stephan Vogel,

Organisers of the First Workshop on Human-Informed Translation and Interpreting Technology (HiT-IT) organised on 7 September 2017 Varna, Bulgaria.

Organizers:

Irina Temnikova, Qatar Computing Research Institute, HBKU, Qatar
Constantin Orăsan, University of Wolverhampton, UK
Gloria Corpas Pastor, University of Malaga, Spain
Stephan Vogel, Qatar Computing Research Institute, HBKU, Qatar

Program Committee:

Ahmed Abdelali, Qatar Computing Research Institute, HBKU, Qatar
Claudio Bendazzoli, Università degli studi di Torino, Italy
Pierrette Bouillon, University of Geneva, Switzerland
Michael Carl, Copenhagen Business School, Denmark
Stephen Doherty, The University of New South Wales, Australia
Claudio Fantinuolli, University of Mainz, Germany
Marcello Federico, Fondazione Bruno Kessler, Trento
Veronique Hoste, University of Ghent, Belgium
Maarit Koponen, University of Turku, Finland
Lieve Macken, University of Ghent, Belgium
Ruslan Mitkov, University of Wolverhampton, UK
Johanna Monti, University of Naples, Italy
Hamdy Mubarak, Qatar Computing Research Institute, HBKU, Qatar
Preslav Nakov, Qatar Computing Research Institute, HBKU, Qatar
Sharon O'Brien, Dublin City University, Ireland
Santanu Pal, Saarland University, Germany
Carla Parra, ADAPT Centre, SALIS, Dublin City University, Ireland
Maja Popovic, Humboldt University of Berlin, Germany
Pablo Romero-Fresco, University of Roehampton, UK
Violeta Seretan, University of Geneva, Switzerland
Cristina Toledo, University of Córdoba, Spain
Victoria Yaneva, University of Wolverhampton, UK
Anna Zaretskaya, University of Malaga, Spain

Invited Speakers:

Ruslan Mitkov, University of Wolverhampton, UK
Preslav Nakov, Qatar Computing Research Institute, HBKU, Qatar

Table of Contents

Conference Program

9:00–9:10	***Workshop opening***
9:10–10:00	*Why are Computers (Still) Bad Translators?* Preslav Nakov (invited speaker)
10:00–10:30	*Enhancing Machine Translation of Academic Course Catalogues with Terminological Resources* Randy Scansani, Silvia Bernardini, Adriano Ferraresi, Federico Gaspari and Marcello Soffritti
10:30–11:00	***Coffee break***
11:00–11:30	*Experiments in Non-Coherent Post-editing* Cristina Toledo Báez, Moritz Schaeffer and Michael Carl
11:30–11:50	*Comparing Machine Translation and Human Translation: A Case Study* Lars Ahrenberg
11:50–12:10	*TransBank: Metadata as the Missing Link between NLP and Traditional Translation Studies* Michael Ustaszewski and Andy Stauder
12:10–12:30	*Interpreting Strategies Annotation in the WAW Corpus* Irina Temnikova, Ahmed Abdelali, Samy Hedaya, Stephan Vogel and Aishah Al Daher
12:30–14:00	***Lunch break***
14:00–14:50	*The Translation World and Beyond... What's Next? Don't Get me Wrong...* Ruslan Mitkov (invited speaker)
14:50–15:10	*Translation Memory Systems Have a Long Way to Go* Andrea Silvestre Baquero and Ruslan Mitkov
15:10–15:30	*Building Dialectal Arabic Corpora* Hani Elgabou and Dimitar Kazakov
15:30–16:00	***Coffee break***

16:00–16:20 *Towards Producing Human-Validated Translation Resources for the Fula language through WordNet Linking*
Khalil Mrini and Martin Benjamin

16:30–17:00 ***Discussion and conclusions***

Enhancing Machine Translation of Academic Course Catalogues with Terminological Resources

Randy Scansani[1]
University of Bologna
Forlì, Italy

Silvia Bernardini[1]
University of Bologna
Forlì, Italy

Adriano Ferraresi[1]
University of Bologna
Forlì, Italy

Federico Gaspari[2]
Università per Stranieri "Dante Alighieri"
Reggio Calabria, Italy

Marcello Soffritti[1]
University of Bologna
Forlì, Italy

[1]name.surname@unibo.it, [2]gaspari@unistrada.it

Abstract

This paper describes an approach to translating course unit descriptions from Italian and German into English, using a phrase-based machine translation (MT) system. The genre is very prominent among those requiring translation by universities in European countries in which English is a non-native language. For each language combination, an in-domain bilingual corpus including course unit and degree program descriptions is used to train an MT engine, whose output is then compared to a baseline engine trained on the Europarl corpus. In a subsequent experiment, a bilingual terminology database is added to the training sets in both engines and its impact on the output quality is evaluated based on BLEU and post-editing score. Results suggest that the use of domain-specific corpora boosts the engines quality for both language combinations, especially for German-English, whereas adding terminological resources does not seem to bring notable benefits.

1 Introduction

1.1 Background

Following the Bologna process, universities have been urged to increase their degree of internationalization, with the aim of creating a European Higher Education Area (EHEA) that encourages students' mobility. This process has brought with it the need of communicating effectively in English also for institutions based in countries where this is not an official language. Nevertheless, previous work has shown that institutional academic communication has not undergone a substantial increase of translated content, both from a qualitative and from a quantitative point of view. Callahan and Herring (2012) claim that the number of universities whose website contents are translated into English varies across the European Union, with Northern and Western countries paying more attention to their internationalization than Southern ones. When quality is in focus, things do not improve: many of the translated documents feature terminological inconsistencies (Candel-Mora and Carrió-Pastor, 2014).

As one of the aims in the creation of the EHEA was to foster students' mobility, availability of multilingual course unit descriptions (or course catalogues) has become especially important. These texts start by indicating the faculty the course belongs to. After this, brief descriptions of the learning outcomes and of the course contents are given. The following sections outline the assessment and teaching methods. Lastly, details are provided regarding the number of ECTS credits for the course unit, useful links and readings for students, information about the lecturer's office hours and the language in which the course is taught.

Several aspects make these texts interesting for our purposes. First, they feature terms that are typical of institutional academic communication, but also expressions that belong to the discipline taught (Ferraresi, 2017). Second, they are usually drafted or translated by teachers and not by professional writers/translators (Fernandez Costales, 2012). Therefore, their disciplinary terminology is likely to be accurate, but they might not comply with the standards of institutional academic communication. Finally, they tend to be repetitive and relatively well-structured, and to be produced in large numbers on a yearly basis, through a mix of drafting from scratch and partial revisions or up-

The Proceedings of the First Workshop on Human-Informed Translation and Interpreting Technology (HiT-IT), pages 1–10,
Varna, Bulgaria, Sept 7, 2017

dates.

These characteristics make course catalogues an ideal test bed for the development of tools supporting translation and terminology harmonization in the institutional academic domain. Indeed, the development of such tools has been on the agenda of universities across Europe for several years now, as testified, e.g., by previous work in this area funded by the EU Commission in 2011 and involving ca. 10 European universities and private companies[1]. Despite its interest, this project does not seem to have undergone substantial development after 2013, nor does it seem to have had the desired impact on the community of stakeholders. In addition to that, it does not include one of our language combinations, i.e. Italian-English.

1.2 Objectives of the Study

In practical terms, being able to automatically translate texts that typically contain expressions belonging to different domains – the academic one and the disciplinary one – raises the question of how to choose the right resources and how to add them to the system in order to improve the output quality and to simplify post-editing. We aim at contributing to machine translation (MT) development not only understanding if MT results for translation in this domain are promising, but also finding out the most effective setup for MT engines, i.e. with a generic corpus, with an in-domain corpus or with one of these corpora and a bilingual glossary belonging to the educational or disciplinary domain.

In addition to focusing on developments for MT and its architecture, we are laying emphasis on MT contribution to the work of post-editors and to translation in the institutional academic domain. The development of an MT tool able to support professional and non-professional post-editors would speed up the translation of texts, thus favoring the internationalization of universities. Moreover, the present study is part of a larger project that aims to test the impact of terminology on output quality, post-editing effort and post-editor satisfaction[2]. Since terminology inconsistencies can negatively affect both output quality and post-editor's trust in an MT system, we are also investigating the relationship (if any) between the use of terminology resources at various stages of the MT-PE pipeline, and the perception of output quality and post-editing effort by professional and non-professional post-editors (Gaspari et al., 2014; Moorkens et al., 2015). To sum up, even if at these initial stages we are primarily interested in discovering the most effective architecture for our MT tool for this peculiar domain, we see these initial steps as crucially related to the overall application in a real-world scenario where human-machine interaction is of the essence.

For this study, a phrase-based statistical machine translation system (PBSMT) was used to translate course unit descriptions from Italian into English and from German into English. We built a baseline engine trained on a subset of the Europarl[3] corpus. Then, a small in-domain corpus including course unit descriptions and degree programs (see sect. 3.2) belonging to the disciplinary domain of the exact sciences was used to build our in-domain engine. We chose to limit our scope and concentrate on exact sciences since German and Italian degree programs whose course units belong to this domain translate their contents into English more often than other programs (the scarcity of high-quality human-translated parallel texts is arguably the major challenge for our work). We enriched the two training data sets with a bilingual terminology database belonging to the educational domain (see sect. 3.3) and we built two new engines: one trained on the Europarl corpus subset plus the bilingual terminology database, and one on the in-domain bilingual sentence pairs plus the bilingual terminology database. Each of the four engines for each language combination was then tuned on a subset of the in-domain corpus (more details about the resources are given in sect. 3). To evaluate the output quality, we are relying on two popular metrics: the widely-used BLEU score (Papineni et al., 2002) and post-editing score. The latter is based on edit-distance, like other popular methods such as TER or HTER (Snover et al., 2006), i.e. on the post-edits required to turn an MT output segment into its human reference. Even if our reference text is not a post-edited translation of the evaluation data set source side, we chose to also consider the PES results since they tend to be more clear for translators and post-editors.

[1] http://www.bologna-translation.eu/

[2] This work is part of a three-year project that will also include experiments with post-editors, aimed at measuring their reactions to machine-translated output enhanced with terminological backup information, as well as tests on neural machine translation (NMT).

[3] http://www.statmt.org/europarl/

2 Previous Work

A number of approaches have already been developed to use in-domain resources like corpora, terminology and multi-word expressions (MWEs) in statistical machine translation (SMT), to tackle the domain-adaptation challenge for MT. For example, the WMT 2007 shared task was focused on domain adaptation in a scenario in which a small in-domain corpus is available and has to be integrated with large generic corpora (Koehn and Schroeder, 2007; Civera and Juan, 2007). More recently, the work by Štajner et al. (2016) addressed the same problem and showed that an English-Portuguese PBSMT system in the IT domain achieved best results when trained on a large generic corpus and in-domain terminology.

Langlais (2002) showed that adding terminology to the phrase-table actually improved the WER score for the French-English combination in the military domain. For the same language combination, Bouamor et al. (2012) used pairs of MWEs extracted from the Europarl corpus as one of the training resources, but only observed a gain of 0.3% BLEU points (Papineni et al., 2002). Ren et al. (2009) extracted domain-specific MWEs from the training corpora showing encouraging improvements in terms of BLEU score for translations from English to Chinese in the patent domain. A sophisticated approach is the one described in Pinnis and Skadins (2012), where terms and named entities are extracted from in-domain corpora and then used as seeds to crawl the web and collect a comparable corpus from which more terms are extracted and then added to the training data. This method shows an improvement of up to 24.1% BLEU points for the English-Latvian combination in the automotive domain.

Methods to integrate terminology in MT have been recently developed focusing on how to dynamically insert terminology into a PBSMT system, i.e. injecting terminology in an MT engine without having to stop it or re-train it. Such methods suit the purpose of the present paper, as they focus (also) on Italian, German and English. Arcan et al. (2014a) tested for the first time the cache-based method (Bertoldi et al., 2013) to inject bilingual terms into a SMT system without having to stop it. This brought to an improvement of up to 15% BLEU score points for English-Italian in medical and IT domains. For the same domains and with the same languages (in both directions), Arcan et al. (2014b) developed an architecture to identify terminology in a source text and translate it using Wikipedia. This study resulted in an improvement of up to 13% BLEU score points. Moving to approaches focusing exclusively on morphologically complex languages, Pinnis (2015) reported on a new pre-processing method for the source text in order to extract terminology, translate it and add it to the MT system. An evaluation for English-German, English-Latvian and English-Lithuanian in the automotive domain showed an improvement of up to 3.41 BLEU points. The manual evaluation pointed out an increase of up to 52.6% in the number of the terms translated correctly.

3 Experimental Setup

3.1 Machine Translation System

The system we used to build the engines for this experiment is the open-source ModernMT (MMT)[4]. MMT (Bertoldi et al., 2017) is a project funded by the European Union which aims to provide translators and enterprises with a new and innovative phrase-based tool. The main reasons behind the choice of this software is that it is able to build custom engines without long and computationally complex training and tuning phases, providing high-quality translations for specific domains. As a matter of fact, recent evaluation (Bertoldi et al., 2017) carried out on texts from 8 different domains and for two language combinations (English-French and English-German), showed that MMT's training and tuning are faster than Moses', while their quality is similar. Besides, MMT outperforms Google Translate when translating texts belonging to specific domains on which the engine was trained.

For this work, we exploited both the tuning and testing procedures already implemented in MMT, i.e. a standard Minimum Error Rate Training (MERT) (Och, 2003) and a testing phase in which the engine can be evaluated on a specific set of data chosen by the user. The metrics used are the BLEU score (Papineni et al., 2002) and the post-editing score (PES), which is the inverse of the TER score (Snover et al., 2006).

3.2 Corpora

As mentioned in sect. 1.2, we enriched a baseline and an in-domain MT system using in-domain cor-

[4] `http://www.modernmt.eu/`

pora and terminology. Due to limitations of the computational resources available, training and tuning an engine on the whole Europarl corpus would not have been possible. We therefore extracted a subset of 300,000 sentence pairs from the Europarl corpus both for Italian-English and for German-English to use them as the training set of our baseline engine. Then, bilingual corpora belonging to the academic domain were needed as in-domain training, development and evaluation data sets for the two language combinations. Relying only on course unit descriptions to train our engines could have led to over-fitting of the models. Also, good-quality bilingual versions of course unit descriptions are often not available. To overcome these two issues we added a small number of degree program descriptions to our in-domain corpora, i.e. texts that are similar to course unit descriptions, but provide general information on a degree program, and are thus less focused on a specific discipline or course.

To build our in-domain corpora, we followed the method developed within the CODE project[5]. An Italian-English corpus of course catalogues was also available thanks to this project. The starting point for the search for institutional academic texts in German and Italian was the University Ranking provided by Webometrics[6]. This website ranks Higher Education Institutions from all over the world based on their web presence and impact. We crawled the top university websites in Italy and Germany and for each of the two countries we identified the four universities with the largest quantity of contents translated into English. From these, we downloaded texts within the exact sciences domain.

For the German-English combination, we collected two bigger corpora of course unit descriptions, and two smaller ones of degree program descriptions. For the Italian-English one we collected a corpus of course unit descriptions and two smaller corpora of degree program descriptions, to which we then added the CODE course unit descriptions corpus after cleaning of texts not belonging to the exact science domain. For both language combinations, each corpus was extracted from a different university website. We ended up with 35,200 segment pairs for German-English and 42,000 for Italian-English. The smallest corpus made of course unit descriptions was used as evaluation data set, i.e. 4,400 sentence pairs out of 35,200 for German-English and 3,700 out of 42,000 for Italian-English. 3,500 sentence pairs from the biggest course unit description corpus were extracted for each of the language combinations to exploit them as development set. The remaining sentence pairs – i.e. 27,300 for German-English and 34,800 for Italian-English – were used as training set for the in-domain engines.

3.3 Terminology

The terminology database was created merging three different IATE (InterActive Terminology for Europe)[7] termbases for both language pairs and adding to them terms and MWEs extracted from the Eurydice[8] glossaries. More specifically, the three different IATE termbases were the following: Education, Teaching, Organization of teaching. We also extracted the monolingual terms from the summary tables at the end of the five Eurydice volumes and we chose to keep just the terms in the fifth volume which are already translated into English and those terms whose translation in the target language was relatively straightforward (for example *Direttore di dipartimento* in Italian and "Head of department" in English).

The three different IATE files were in xml format and their terms were grouped based on their underlying concepts, so a single entry often contained more than one source term related to many target terms. For example one entry included the German terms *Erziehung und Unterricht* and *Unterricht und Erziehung*, that are translated into English as "educational services", "instruction services", "teaching" and "tuition". We extracted each term pair and merged them into a single plain-text (tab separated) bilingual termbase, where each pair has its own entry. We then collected the Eurydice bilingual terms and merged them with those extracted from IATE. At the end of this process, we obtained an Italian-English termbase with 4,143 bilingual entries and a German-English one with 5,465 bilingual entries.

In order to test the relevance of our term collec-

[5]CODE is a project aimed at building corpora and tools to support translation of course unit descriptions into English and drafting of these texts in English as a lingua franca. http://code.sslmit.unibo.it/doku.php

[6]http://www.webometrics.info/en

[7]http://iate.europa.eu/

[8]http://eacea.ec.europa.eu/education/eurydice/

tions for the experiment, we computed the number of types and tokens of the evaluation data set on the source side, and the number of termbase entries. We then compared these figures to the degree of overlap between the two resources, i.e. tokens and types occurring both in the termbase and in the source side of the evaluation data set for both language pairs, so as to gauge the relevance of the termbase. Since our termbase does not contain any inflected form, we are computing the degree of overlap only on the canonical form of the terms. Results are displayed in Tables 1 and 2.

It-En	
Corpus tokens	50,248
Corpus types	6,985
Termbase entries	4,142
Tokens overlap	20.44%
Types overlap	13.27%

Table 1: Types and tokens in the evaluation data sets, termbase entries, and type/token overlap between the two resources for It-En.

De-En	
Corpus tokens	26,956
Corpus types	5,614
Termbase entries	5,462
Tokens overlap	19.98%
Types overlap	9.63%

Table 2: Types and tokens in the evaluation data sets, termbase entries, and type/token overlap between the two resources for De-En.

The German-English corpus tokens are half those in the Italian-English corpus, while the Italian-English corpus includes ca. 1,300 types more than the German-English one (approximately 20% of the total number of Italian types). When German is the source language, the number of termbase entries is ca. one fifth of the corpus tokens, while the number of the Italian-English glossary entries is only one twelfth of the number of corpus tokens. The ratio between number of overlapping tokens and number of corpus tokens remains the same across the two language combinations (ca. 20%), while the ratio related to types is 13.27% for Italian-English and 9.63% for German-English. Based on these figures, we would expect our Italian-English termbase to have a slightly stronger influence on the output than the German-English one.

It is also interesting to observe the list of the glossary words occurring in the output ranked by their frequency for both source languages. For German the first five are *Informatik*, *Software*, *Vorlesung*, *Fakultät*, *Studium*, while for Italian we have: *corso*, *insegnamento*, *calcolo*, *prova*, *voto*. Considering the low degree of overlap and the large presence of basic words for the domain in both languages – and since most of them are unlikely to have multiple translations – we decided not to work on a time-demanding task such as solving the ambiguities in the termbase.

4 Experimental Results

For both language combinations we used MMT to create four engines:

- One engine trained on the subset of Europarl (baseline).
- One engine trained on the subset of Europarl and the terminology database (baseline+terms).
- One engine trained on the in-domain corpora (in-domain).
- One engine trained on the in-domain corpora and the terminology database (in-domain+terms).

Each engine was then tuned on a development set formed of 3,500 in-domain sentence pairs and evaluated on ca. 3,700 segment pairs (for Italian-English) and 4,400 segment couples (for German-English) (see sect. 3.2 for a description of the training, tuning and testing data sets).

4.1 Italian-English

For the engine that translates from Italian into English, results are shown in Table 3. If we compare the best in-domain engine to the best baseline according to the BLEU score, we can see that, after the tuning phase, the in-domain engine outperforms the baseline+terms by 7.85 points. Moreover, each engine has improved its performance according to both metrics after being tuned on our development set.

According to the automatic metrics, and contrary to our expectations, adding the terminology database did not influence the in-domain engines or the baseline ones in a substantial way, sometimes actually causing a slight decrease in the engine performance. For example, our two in-domain engines had similar performance both before tuning – when their scores differed by 0.22 BLEU points and 0.19 PES points, with the in-domain outperforming its counterpart with terminology – and after tuning, when in-domain outperformed in-domain+terms by 0.78 BLEU points and 0.35 PES points.

To gain a slightly better insight into the engine performance, we quickly analyzed the outputs of the four engines. Many sentences contained untranslated words or word-order issues. The reference sentence "During the semester, two guided visits to relevant experimental workshops on the topics covered in the course will be organized" contained the words "semester" and "course" that are basic words of the domain and appear in the glossary. However, in both baseline engines the output is "During the half, will be organized two visits led to experimental laboratories relevant to the subjects raised during" and in both the in-domain ones the output is "During the semester, will be two visits to experimental laboratories pertinent to topics covered in the course". Two things are interesting here. First of all, the output confirms what the automatic metrics already highlighted: the output of the engines without terms is generally very similar to the output with terms. Moreover, adding the termbase did not substantially improve the generic output even when some of its words appeared in the termbase. We will discuss these results further in sect. 4.3.

It-En Engine	BLEU	PES
Baseline	16.90	35.27
Baseline tuned	22.58	40.08
Baseline+terms	17.09	35.04
Baseline+terms tuned	**22.75**	**40.36**
In-domain	26.72	50.61
In-domain tuned	**30.60**	**53.17**
In-domain+terms	26.50	50.42
In-domain+terms tuned	29.82	52.82

Table 3: Results for the Italian-English combination. For each engine, BLEU and PES scores are given both before and after tuning. The best baseline and in-domain results are shown in bold.

De-En Engine	BLEU	PES
Baseline	24.03	41.24
Baseline tuned	34.98	47.70
Baseline+terms	25.65	42.10
Baseline+terms tuned	**36.89**	**49.03**
In-domain	43.21	49.06
In-domain tuned	46.31	50.75
In-domain+terms	43.48	49.23
In-domain+terms tuned	**47.05**	**51.20**

Table 4: Results for the German-English combination. For each engine, BLEU and PES scores are given both before and after tuning. The best baseline and in-domain results are shown in bold.

4.2 German-English

Table 4 shows results for the German-English language combination. After tuning, the best in-domain engine outperformed the baseline by 10.16 points according to BLEU and by 2.17 points according to PES. The tuning performed on the in-domain engines causes an improvement of more than 3% in terms of BLEU score. Regarding the baseline engines, the tuning enhances the quality by ca. 10 BLEU points and 7 PES points, thus narrowing the performance gap between the two different kinds of engines.

What is important to notice is that, counter-intuitively and similarly to what we observed for the Italian-English combination, the collection of academic terminology does not affect the translation output quality: the metrics show an improvement of 0.74 BLEU points and 0.45 PES points when terminology is added to the in-domain engine (results after the tuning phase). The addition of terminology seems to be slightly more effective on the baseline engines, improving the automatic scores by 1.91 BLEU points and 1.33 PES points after tuning.

A quick analysis of the output shows the same issues identified in sect. 4.1. One example is the reference sentence "Lecture, exercises, programming exercises for individual study", that is translated as "Lecture, exercises, Programmieraufgaben zum private study" in both in-domain engines and as "Lecture, exercise, Programmieraufgaben on Selbststudium" in both baseline engines (the word couple *Vorlesung*-Lecture was in the termbase). The same German word was not translated in some sentences of the two in-domain engines outputs – e.g. "Vorlesung (presentation of

Slides and presentation interactive examples)", for the engine with terms and "Vorlesung (presentation of presentation and interaktiver examples)" for the engine without terms – while it was in the baseline ones: "Lecture (presentation of Folien and idea interactive examples)". This is another negative result for our termbase, since neither of the in-domain engines translated "Vorlesung" as "lecture", while the baseline ones did without the help of the terminological resource. We will further discuss these results in sect. 4.3.

4.3 Discussion

In our experimental setup, adding terminology to a general-purpose engine and to an in-domain engine does not influence the output quality substantially. We compared the figures in Tables 1 and 2 (regarding the degree of overlap between the evaluation data set and the bilingual glossary) to the automatic scores assigned to our engines (Tables 3 and 4) to investigate the impact on output quality. The degree of tokens overlap between the bilingual glossary and the evaluation data set is similar for the two source languages (ca. 20%). Despite this, for the German-English combination the baseline+terms engine outperformed the baseline engine by 1.91 BLEU points and 1.33 PES points, which is the largest gain obtained in this study adding a bilingual glossary to the training data set. If we look at the baseline and baseline+terms engines for Italian-English, for example, the latter outperformed the former by only 0.17 BLEU and 0.28 PES points. This might suggest that the target terms in the German-English glossary were consistent with those used in the reference text, while for Italian-English there were more discrepancies between the two resources.

Another variable that has to be taken into account is the way in which terms are extracted and injected into the MT engine. As reported in sect. 2, methods in which terminology is extracted from other resources and then added to training data sets (Bouamor et al., 2012) are less effective than, for example, approaches in which terminology is extracted from the training data set (Ren et al., 2009; Pinnis and Skadinš, 2012) or injected dynamically, i.e. at run-time without re-training, into the MT engine (Arcan et al., 2014a). In our case the Italian-English term pairs were 4,143 against the 34,800 sentence pairs of the training data set, while for German-English we had 5,465 term pairs as compared to 27,300 sentence pairs. Due to the difference in the amount of term pairs and segment pairs, simply adding the glossary to the sentence pairs might cause it to lose its influence on the training process.

If we look at Tables 3 and 4, we can see that in-domain segments boost the engine quality both during training – with the in-domain engines outperforming the baseline – and after tuning, which brings remarkable improvements. This could suggest that the PBSMT system is able to extract academic terms and expressions from the in-domain corpus, without the need of being enhanced with a termbase belonging to the same domain. Additional evidence for this are the examples in section 4.1, where some of the termbase words were not translated in the baseline engines output of both language combinations, while they were correctly translated in both in-domain engines. As a matter of fact, the terminology database was able to increase the score by more than 1% in terms of BLEU only on one occasion – i.e. the baseline engine for German-English –, while for the other three engine pairs (in-domain with and without terms for German-English, baseline and in-domain with and without terms for Italian-English) the performance increased by few decimals or even decreased. The same happens if we look at the PES score.

To further discuss the results without using the BLEU metric, whose figures are often less intuitive than the PES' ones especially for translators and post-editors, it is interesting to notice how the in-domain engines for both language combinations always reach at least 50% in terms of PES score after tuning. Despite the low quality of the examples seen in sections 4.1 and 4.2, these PES scores are an encouraging result if we consider that we are carrying out the first experiment on this domain and that we are exploiting quite a small amount of in-domain resources to build our engine, a condition that is likely to remain constant given the nature of communication in this domain. It also suggests that, in this domain, MT is likely to boost the post-editor's productivity if compared to a translation from scratch. Moreover, we expect to obtain further improvements building an engine combining both generic and in-domain resources in the training phase, so as to hopefully observe a further increase of the PES and hence of the post-editor productivity.

5 Conclusion and Further Work

This paper has described an attempt at evaluating the potential of the use of in-domain resources (terminology and corpora) with MT in the institutional academic domain, and more precisely for the translation of course unit descriptions from German into English and from Italian into English. Following the results of the present experiment, we are planning to carry out further work in this field.

Since academic terms are only one subset of the terminology used in course unit descriptions, which also includes terms related to the subject matter of each unit, it would be interesting to investigate the advantages of adding disciplinary terminology alongside the academic one. We therefore plan to combine academic and disciplinary terminology. Following the encouraging results of the baseline engine tuned on the in-domain resources, we also plan to investigate the performance of an engine trained on both generic and in-domain resources and tuned on an in-domain development set. As shown in the work by Štajner et al. (2016), PBSMT systems' performance increases when the training data set includes a small quantity of in-domain resources – corpora or termbase – and a large generic corpus.

As we have seen in section 3.3 the overlap afforded by the termbase used for this experiment was less than optimal and its structure would require an accurate procedure to extract the most likely term pair for this domain, since a source term often has multiple target translations. For these reasons and basing on the results, IATE is probably not the best resource for our purposes. As part of future work, we are interested in extracting terminology from other resources, e.g. the UCL-K.U.Leuven University Terminology Database[9], or, ideally, from a resource developed collaboratively by universities across Europe, consistent with EU-wide terminological efforts but more readily usable and focusing on agreed-upon terms and with limited ambiguity. We will also test methods to make available the most relevant terms for the texts to be translated, i.e. extracting terminology from the training data. In both cases – use of external resources or extraction from the training data set – we are planning to add inflected forms of the terms. In addition to their extraction, we are considering injection of terms into an MT system in other ways than simply adding them to the training set, where the termbase is likely to play a minor role because of its small size compared to the corpora. In future work we will compare methods to add terms at run-time in a post-editing environment, in order to analyze the impact of these suggestions on the post-editors' work. What we are expecting from this experiment is to find a way to increase the post-editor trust in the suggested terminology, and hence in the MT engine.

As this was our first attempt to build an MT engine in this domain, sometimes we were forced to concentrate on more technical aspects, e.g. the improvements in the BLEU score to analyze the engines' development. In future work we are planning to use metrics that better take into account terminology translation (e.g. precision, recall, f-measure) and also manual evaluation to collect more data on the impact of our work on the post-editing phase.

To conclude, in this paper we have taken a first step toward the development of a tool that combines machine translation, corpora and terminology databases, with the aim of streamlining the provision of course unit descriptions in English by European universities. Our in-domain engines showed encouraging results, even if – as expected – they are not able to boost a post-editor's productivity yet, while the role of terminology (what kind, how it is injected into the engine) is still to be further investigated, as is the confidence-building potential of quality terminology databases on post-editing work.

[9]`https://sites.uclouvain.be/lexique/lexique.php`

Acknowledgments

The authors would like to thank Mauro Cettolo, Marcello Federico and Luisa Bentivogli of Fondazione Bruno Kessler (FBK) for their advice and for help with ModernMT, and three anonymous reviews for insightful comments on the first draft of this paper. The usual disclaimers apply.

References

Mihael Arcan, Claudio Giuliano, Marco Turchi, and Paul Buitelaar. 2014b. Identification of bilingual terms from monolingual documents for statistical machine translation. In *Proceedings of the 4th International Workshop on Computa-*

tional Terminology. Dublin, Ireland, pages 22–31. http://www.aclweb.org/anthology/W14-4803.

Mihael Arcan, Marco Turchi, Sara Tonelli, and Paul Buitelaar. 2014a. Enhancing statistical machine translation with bilingual terminology in a CAT environment. In Yaser Al-Onaizan and Michel Simard, editors, *Proceedings of AMTA 2014*. Vancouver, BC.

Nicola Bertoldi, Roldano Cattoni, Mauro Cettolo, Amin Farajian, Marcello Federico, Davide Caroselli, Luca Mastrostefano, Andrea Rossi, Marco Trombetti, Ulrich Germann, and David Madl. 2017. MMT: New open source MT for the translation industry. In *Proceedings of the 20th Annual Conference of the European Association for Machine Translation*. Prague, pages 86–91. https://ufal.mff.cuni.cz/eamt2017/user-project-product-papers/papers/user/EAMT2017_paper_88.pdf.

Nicola Bertoldi, Mauro Cettolo, and Marcello Federico. 2013. Cache-based online adaptation for machine translation enhanced computer assisted translation. In Andy Way, Khalil Sima'an, Mikel L. Forcada, Daniel Grasmick, and Heidi Depaetere, editors, *Proceedings of the XIV Machine Translation Summit*. Nice, France, pages 35–42.

Dhouha Bouamor, Nasredine Semmar, and Pierre Zweigenbaum. 2012. Identifying bilingual multi-word expressions for statistical machine translation. In Nicoletta Calzolari, Khalid Choukri, Thierry Declerck, Mehmet Uğur Doğan, Bente Maegaard, Joseph Mariani, Jan Odijk, and Stelios Piperidis, editors, *Proceedings of the Eighth International Conference on Language Resources and Evaluation (LREC-2012)*. European Language Resources Association (ELRA), Istanbul, Turkey, pages 674–679. ACL Anthology Identifier: L12-1527. http://www.lrec-conf.org/proceedings/lrec2012/pdf/886_Paper.pdf.

Ewa Callahan and Susan C. Herring. 2012. Language choice on university websites: Longitudinal trends. *Journal of International Communication* 6 (2012):322–355.

Miguel Ángel Candel-Mora and María Luisa Carrió-Pastor. 2014. Terminology standardization strategies towards the consolidation of the European Higher Education Area. *Procedia - Social and Behavioral Sciences* 116:166 – 171.

Jorge Civera and Alfons Juan. 2007. Domain adaptation in statistical machine translation with mixture modelling. In *Proceedings of the Second Workshop on Statistical Machine Translation*. Association for Computational Linguistics, Prague, Czech Republic, pages 177–180. http://www.aclweb.org/anthology/W/W07/W07-0222.

Alberto Fernandez Costales. 2012. The internationalization of institutional websites. In Anthony Pym and David Orrego-Carmona, editors, *Translation Research Projects*. Tarragona: Intercultural Studies Group, pages 51–60.

Adriano Ferraresi. 2017. Terminology in European university settings. The case of course unit descriptions. In Paola Faini, editor, *Terminological Approaches in the European Context*. Cambridge Scholars Publishing, Newcastle upon Tyne, pages 20–40.

Federico Gaspari, Antonio Toral, Sudip Kumar Naskar, Declan Groves, and Andy Way. 2014. Perception vs reality: Measuring machine translation post-editing productivity. In Sharon O'Brien, Michel Simard, and Lucia Specia, editors, *Proceedings of AMTA 2014*. Vancouver, BC, pages 60–72.

Philipp Koehn and Josh Schroeder. 2007. Experiments in domain adaptation for statistical machine translation. In *Proceedings of the Second Workshop on Statistical Machine Translation*. Association for Computational Linguistics, Prague, StatMT '07, pages 224–227. http://dl.acm.org/citation.cfm?id=1626355.1626388.

Philippe Langlais. 2002. Improving a general-purpose statistical translation engine by terminological lexicons. In *COLING-02 on COMPUTERM 2002: Second International Workshop on Computational Terminology - Volume 14*. Association for Computational Linguistics, Stroudsburg, PA, USA, COMPUTERM '02, pages 1–7. https://doi.org/10.3115/1118771.1118776.

Joss Moorkens, Sharon O'Brien, Igor A. L. da Silva, Norma B. de Lima Fonseca, and Fábio Alves. 2015. Correlations of perceived post-editing effort with measurements of actual effort. *Machine Translation* 29(3-4):267–284.

Franz Josef Och. 2003. Minimum error rate training in statistical machine translation. In *Proceedings of the 41st Annual Meeting of the Association for Computational Linguistics - Volume 1*. Association for Computational Linguistics, Stroudsburg, PA, USA, ACL '03, pages 160–167. https://doi.org/10.3115/1075096.1075117.

Kishore Papineni, Salim Roukos, Todd Ward, and Wei-Jing Zhu. 2002. Bleu: A method for automatic evaluation of machine translation. In *Proceedings of the 40th Annual Meeting of the Association for Computational Linguistics*. Association for Computational Linguistics, Philadelphia, Pennsylvania, ACL '02, pages 311–318. https://doi.org/10.3115/1073083.1073135.

Mārcis Pinnis. 2015. Dynamic terminology integration methods in statistical machine translation. In *Proceedings of the 18th Annual Conference of the European Association for Machine Translation*. Antalya, Turkey, pages 89–96.

Mārcis Pinnis and Raivis Skadinš. 2012. MT adaptation for under-resourced domains - what works and what not. In *Human Language Technologies - The Baltic Perspective - Proceedings of the Fifth International Conference Baltic HLT 2012*. Tartu, Estonia, pages 176–184.

Zhixiang Ren, Yajuan Lü, Jie Cao, Qun Liu, and Yun Huang. 2009. Improving statistical machine translation using domain bilingual multiword expressions. In *Proceedings of the Workshop on Multiword Expressions: Identification, Interpretation, Disambiguation and Applications*. Association for Computational Linguistics, Suntec, Singapore, MWE '09, pages 47–54.

Matthew Snover, Bonnie Dorr, Richard Schwartz, Linnea Micciulla, and John Makhoul. 2006. A study of translation edit rate with targeted human annotation. In *Proceedings of Association for Machine Translation in the Americas*. Cambridge, Massachussets, pages 223–231.

Sanja Štajner, Andreia Querido, Nuno Rendeiro, João António Rodrigues, and António Branco. 2016. Use of domain-specific language resources in machine translation. In Nicoletta Calzolari, Khalid Choukri, Thierry Declerck, Sara Goggi, Marko Grobelnik, Bente Maegaard, Joseph Mariani, Helene Mazo, Asuncion Moreno, Jan Odijk, and Stelios Piperidis, editors, *Proceedings of the Tenth International Conference on Language Resources and Evaluation (LREC 2016)*. European Language Resources Association (ELRA), Paris, France, pages 592–598.

Experiments in Non-Coherent Post-editing

Mª Cristina Toledo Báez
University of Córdoba, Plaza del Cardenal Salazar 3, 14003 Córdoba, Spain
cristina.toledo@uco.es
Moritz Schaeffer
University of Mainz, An der Hochschule 2, 76726 Germersheim, Germany
mschaeffer@uni-mainz.de
Michael Carl
Renmin University, 59 Zhongguancun St, Haidian Qu, China, 100872
Copenhagen Business School, Dalgas Have 15, 2000 Frederiksberg, Denmark
mc.isv@cbs.dk

Abstract

Market pressure on translation productivity joined with technological innovation is likely to fragment and decontextualise translation jobs even more than is currently the case. Many different translators increasingly work on one document at different places, collaboratively working in the cloud. This paper investigates the effect of decontextualised source texts on behaviour by comparing post-editing of sequentially ordered sentences with shuffled sentences from two different texts. The findings suggest that there is little or no effect of the decontextualised source texts on behaviour.

1 Introduction

Machine Translation (MT) has made tremendous progress in the past two decades, first since the introduction of statistical approaches (Brown et al., 1988) and more recently with the emergence of neural-based approaches, also referred to as neural MT (NMT) (e.g., Wu et al., 2016). Klubička et al. (2017) have found that NMT reduces the amount of errors in the translation produced (for news content type, English-to-Croatian) by 54%, as compared to SMT.

Despite the tremendous increase of MT quality in the past years, post-editing of MT output (PEMT) remains a compulsory activity if the translation product is to be used for dissemination. However, better MT output leads to quicker post-editing cycles and increases productivity and efficiency (Specia, 2011). Thus, the even better quality of NMT output is likely to be well suited for post-editing, as it reaches an unprecedented degree of fluency (Toral, 2017)

In a typical PEMT scenario, a human post-editor corrects the translation generated by an MT system. For instance, many translation memory systems (Trados, MemoQ, OmegaT, etc.) provide access to MT systems, the output of which may be merged into the set of translation proposals that are retrieved from the translation base of the TM system.

Recently, the possibility of active learning and active interaction has emerged (Ortiz-Martínez, 2016; Martínez-Gómez et al., 2012; Peris et al., 2016), in which an MT system re-orders the source language segments to be translated and post-edited so as to maximise productivity and the learning effect. Instead of presenting a text in its original sequential order, the system sorts the segments according to a degree of confidence, so that it can learn most (quickly) from the human corrections. This comes along with novel conceptualizations of the translation workflow which link these new possibilities with innovative usage of crowdsourcing. In order to fully exploit the potential in crowdsourcing, novel ways need be found to split up coherent texts into units that can be translated and edited independently by a large number of translators at the same time. Due to the increased demand for translation productivity and shorter translation turnaround, some translation tools (Wordbee, Trados, MATECAT) offer collaborative functionalities. Some LSP companies (Unbabel[1], MotaWord[2]) are seeking possibilities to experiment with a more dynamic approach to collaborative translation that segments a document into smaller units. MotaWord, for instance, declares to be "The World's

[1] https://unbabel.com/ [17.6. 2017]

[2] https://www.motaword.com [17.6. 2017]

The Proceedings of the First Workshop on Human-Informed Translation and Interpreting Technology (HiT-IT), pages 11–20,
Varna, Bulgaria, Sept 7, 2017

Fastest Human Translation Platform" which is based on a collaborative cloud platform "coordinated efficiently through a smart back end" in which over 9,000 translators participate. This is only possible if large documents are split into small segments and by deploying the crowd to post-edit a limited number smaller units. However, it is unclear how translators cope with a situation in which smaller segments - possibly from different parts of the same document - are presented out of context. The impact on translation behaviour has, to our knowledge, never been studied if translators translate segments in a non-sequential order.

In this paper, we investigate the translation processes of post-editors when dealing with segments in a randomized order. We observe translators' post-editing behaviour using research methods (eye tracking and key-logging) and metrics known in the research field of Translation Process Research. Dragsted (2004:32) points out that, from a prescriptive perspective, the translation unit can be considered "the most appropriate segment for establishing SL/TL equivalence" (see, among others, Vinay and Darbelnet, 1995; Catford, 1965; Bell, 1991). From a descriptive, cognitive-oriented perspective, Dragsted (2004:32) argues that the translation unit can also be described "as the segment actually processed, [...] identified on the basis of cognitive processes observable (indirectly) in a set of data." What constitutes the ideal translation unit has received considerable attention: there are several proposals for a cognitively or linguistically plausible unit (e.g. Dragsted 2005, 2006; Carl and Kay 2011; Jakobsen 2011; Alves and Gonçalves 2013). However, for the purpose of this study, and practical reasons, we define a translation unit as a sentence (segment) as demarcated by full stops.

2 Experimental Setup

16 Translation students and 4 professional translators post-edited four English texts into Spanish. The texts were taken from the TPR-DB multiLing[3] corpus. Two of the texts were news texts (Text 1 and 3) and two texts were taken from a sociological encyclopaedia (Texts 5 and 6). Every source text (henceforth ST) had between 122 and 160 words (5-11 segments) and all four texts were machine translated using google translate, as of June 2016 and post-edited. One news text and one sociological text were presented in the original coherent form, and two texts were composed of mixed sentences from the two other texts. Translog-II (Carl 2012) was used as a post-editing tool. A line break separated each new segment in the source and the target side. In total, 80 post-edited texts were collected: 40 posteditions (284 segments) in the mixed-segment mode, and 40 posteditions (284 segments) in the coherent translation mode.

Table 1 shows the mean total duration per post-edited text (*Dur*) in minutes in the two conditions (P=coherent mode, Pm=mixed mode), for the orientation, the drafting and the revision phases. *TrtS* is the total time spent reading the ST and *TrtT* is the total time spent reading the target text (henceforth TT), also in minutes. Deletions and Insertions are counted in characters. It is obvious from the means that the order in which the segments are shown has little (in the case of insertions and deletions) effect or no effect on average values.

Task	**Total Duration**	**Orientation**
P	5.97 (4.21)	0.53 (0.47)
Pm	5.69 (2.70)	0.53 (0.43)
P	**Draft**	**Revision**
Pm	4.58 (3.43)	0.86 (0.94)
	4.50 (2.28)	0.65 (0.71)
	TrtS	**TrtT**
P	1.46 (1.12)	3.72 (2.87)
Pm	1.44 (0.74)	3.39 (1.86)
	Deletions	**Insertions**
P	125 (61)	134 (73)
Pm	142 (60)	144 (65)

Table 1: descriptive statistics for the data: means and standard deviation in parentheses.

3 Translation Difficulty Indicator

Mishra et al (2013) develop a Translation Difficulty Index (TDI) which aims at predicting the effort during translation, measured in terms of the sum of ST and TT reading times (TDI score). They show that the TDI score correlates with the degree of polysemy, structural complexity and length of ST segments. They train a Support Vector Machine on observed eye movement data and predicted the

[3] https://sites.google.com/site/centretranslationinnovation/tpr-db

TDI score of unseen data during translation on the basis of the linguistic features.

The segments in the mixed post-editing mode were ordered according to the Translation Difficulty Indicator (TDI) (Mishra et al., 2013), ordering from the highest to the lowest TDI. The texts which resulted from merging two texts were then split up again into two texts which were post-edited independently from each other. This resulted in one text each with an overall higher TDI score and one with an overall lower TDI score, given that the segments in the merged text had been ordered by the TDI score from high to low. Texts were presented in a pseudo-randomized order, but post-editors had to post-edit first the two coherent texts and then the two texts in the mixed mode.

Table 2 shows how the segments were order in the mixed mode. *STseg* is the number in the sequential order in which the ST segments were shown to post-editors. *Text* is the unique identifier for the texts. In this case, there are two merged texts: Text 35 is composed of the segments from the original texts 3 and 5 - Otext shows the text to which the segments originally belong. *OSTseg* shows the sequential numbering of the original (not mixed) texts. The segments in the mixed texts are ordered according to the TDI score (minor adjustments were made to avoid that two segments were shown in the original sequential order).

STseg	Text	Otext	OSTseg	TDI
1	53	5	2	4.11
2	53	3	1	4.02
3	53	5	5	3.3
4	53	3	5	2.82
5	53	5	1	3.16
6	53	5	6	3.3

Table 2: Ordering of segments in the mixed post-editing mode

4 Aims and Method

It is the aim of the current study is to investigate whether text level coherence has an effect on production speed in general and on eye movement behaviour and cognitive effort in particular. In other words, it is the aim to find out whether presenting segments belonging to two different texts in a relatively random order has an effect on cognitive effort.

For all the analyses in the present study, R (R Development Core Team, 2014) and the lme4 (Bates et al., 2014) and languageR (Baayen 2013) packages were used to perform linear mixed-effects models (LMEMs). To test for significance, the R package lmerTest (Kuznetsova et al., 2014) was used. The R^2 for LMEMs was calculated with the MuMIn package (Bartoń 2009). Data that were more than 2.5 standard deviations below or above the participant's mean for the individual measure were excluded from analyses. All the LMEMs had participant and item as random variables.

5 The Effect of Text Level Coherence on Behaviour

For the effect of text level coherence on production duration, the scaled and centred typing duration per segment (*Dur*) was used as dependent variable. The dependent variable was scaled and centred, because the predictors were on very different scales. The variable *Dur* is defined by the keystrokes belonging to a given sentence. It does not include the time that elapses between the last keystroke of the previous sentence and the first keystroke of the current sentence, but it does include any pauses between keystrokes belonging to the same sentence. Given that participants were post-editing, a segment can have a typing duration of zero if the participant did not change anything in the MT output. All potentially relevant variables were entered as predictors in the LMEMs and those which were not significant were excluded. The final model for production duration per segment (*Dur*) had the following predictors: word translation entropy (*HTra*), the number of insertions (*ins*) in characters, Task (post-editing a text in coherent order (*P*) and in the mixed mode (*Pm*)), sequential numbering of the segments as they were shown to participants (*STseg*), the total reading time on the source and target segments, i.e. the total time a particular source segment (*TrtS*) or target segment (*TrtT*) was read, how often the typing was not in a sequential order, i.e. how often the post-editor typed successive keystrokes which were part of two or more different words (*Scatter*) and the number of times a segment has been edited (*Nedit*). Word translation entropy (*HTra*) describes the number of lexical (word translation) choices for the final TTs - the smaller the *HTra* value, the less lexical choices a translator has in the final target sentence (cf. Carl et al. (2016) for a detailed description of this metric).

HTra had a relatively large and significant positive effect on *Dur* (see Table 3): more translation choices induce longer translation times. The effect of the number of insertions was expectedly large, positive and significant. As would be expected, total reading time on the source (*TrtS*) and on the target (*TrtT*) had both very large and highly significant effects. Both *Scatter* and *Nedit* had relatively large significant effects on typing duration (*Dur*).

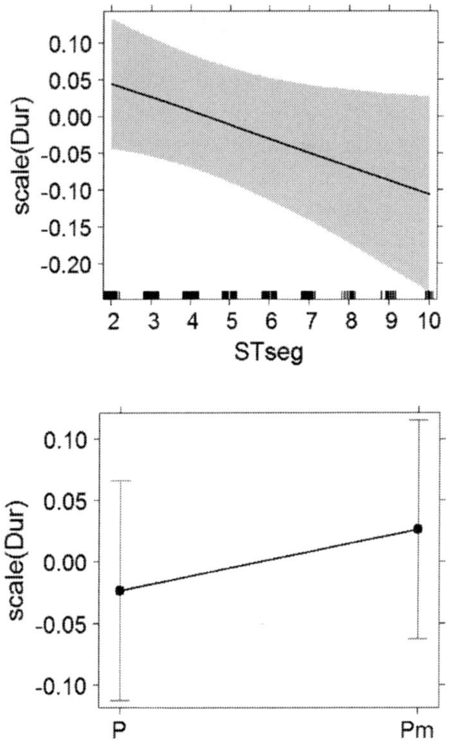

Figure 1: The effect of *Task* and sequential numbering of source segments (*STseg*) on typing duration (*Dur*).

Both *Scatter* and *Nedit* are indicators of revision behaviour suggesting faulty MT output. The Task (coherent versus mixed mode) had no significant effect on typing duration (*Dur*). This result was surprising, given that it could be expected to be more effortful to process a text where segments from two different texts are jumbled in one text. The marginally significant, negative and modest effect of the sequential numbering of segments (*STseg*) (see Figure 1) would have been expected if post-editors had only worked in the coherent mode, since it could be argued that post-editors become more familiar with the topic, the semantic fields and other aspects of the ST and target language as they progress through the text. Schaeffer et al. (2016) show that *STseg* has a facilitating effect on all relevant eye movement measures during from scratch translation and argue that translators create a text level coherence model which makes translation less effortful and the TT more predictable. In the mixed post-editing mode, it is arguably more difficult to create a text level coherence model which would facilitate the process. However, when the interaction between Task and *STseg* was not even approaching significance (β=-0.04, SE= 0.05, *t*= -0.76, $p < 0.450$). What these results suggest is that both the finding in Schaeffer et al. (2016) and the effect of *STseg* on behaviour is not dependent on textual coherence, but is related to a task facilitation effect - the longer the task is carried out, the easier it becomes. The model for typing duration (*Dur*) without interaction provided a very good fit (marginal $R^2 = 0.74$, conditional $R^2= 0.77$).

In order to investigate the reading behaviour on the ST, *TrtS* (the sum total of all fixation durations on an ST segment) was used as dependent variable. *TrtS* was log-transformed because it was not normally distributed. The predictors were the number of tokens in the ST segment (*TokS*), word translation entropy (*HTra*), the number of deletions per

Predictor	*β*	SE	*t*	*p*	
HTra	0.09	0.03	2.75	0.007	**
ins	0.15	0.05	3.34	0.001	***
TaskPm	0.05	0.05	1.08	0.282	
STseg	-0.05	0.02	-1.93	0.055	.
TrtS	0.27	0.03	10.65	<2e-16	***
TrtT	0.42	0.03	13.43	<2e-16	***
Scatter	0.13	0.04	2.98	0.003	**
Nedit	0.06	0.02	2.27	0.024	*

Table 3: The LMEM for typing duration (*Dur*).

segment (*del*), and finally Task and *STseg*. No other variables had a significant effect on *TrtS*.

TokS had an expectedly large positive and highly significant effect on *TrtS* (see Table 4). *HTra* also had a relatively large, positive and highly significant effect *TrtS*. This effect has been observed pre-

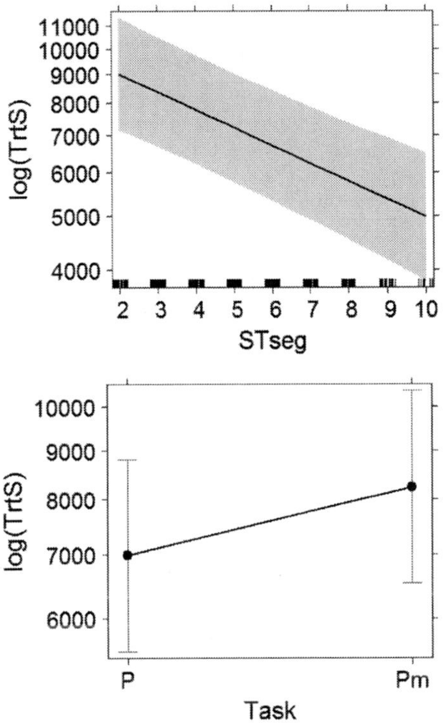

Figure 2:The effect of *Task* and sequential numbering of source segments (*STseg*) on total reading time on the ST (*TrtS*).

viously for from-scratch translation (Schaeffer et al., 2016a) and simply shows that the less literal a translation is, the more cognitive effort is required to arrive at a TT. The number of deletions had a large, positive and significant effect on *TrtS*. Task had a modest, positive and significant effect on *TrtS*, while *STseg* had a large, negative and highly significant effect on *TrtS* (see Figure 2). Again, the fact that the effect of *STseg* was so large, highly significant and negative was surprising, given that half the texts were post-edited in the mixed mode and it could be argued that it is very difficult to develop a text level coherence model in this mode. The interaction between Task and *STseg* was not significant (see Figure 3), suggesting that the *STseg* effect is a task facilitation effect in both tasks and that this effect is very similar in both tasks. However, text level coherence did have an effect on *TrtS*, suggesting that the lack of coherence requires a modest amount of additional effort when reading the ST. The model for total reading time on the ST (*TrtS*) without interaction provided a relatively good fit (marginal $R^2 = 0.32$, conditional $R^2 = 0.63$).

Rather than looking only at the absolute time participants spent reading the TT, we also investigated the effect of text level coherence on the percentage of the total reading time participants (*TrtS*

Predictor	β	SE	t	p	
TokS	0.44	0.05	8.57	4.12E-10	***
HTra	0.16	0.05	3.50	0.001	***
del	0.11	0.04	3.11	0.002	**
TaskPm	0.16	0.06	2.85	0.005	**
STseg	-0.18	0.03	-5.81	1.31E-08	***

Table 4: The LMEM for total reading time on the ST (*TrtS*)

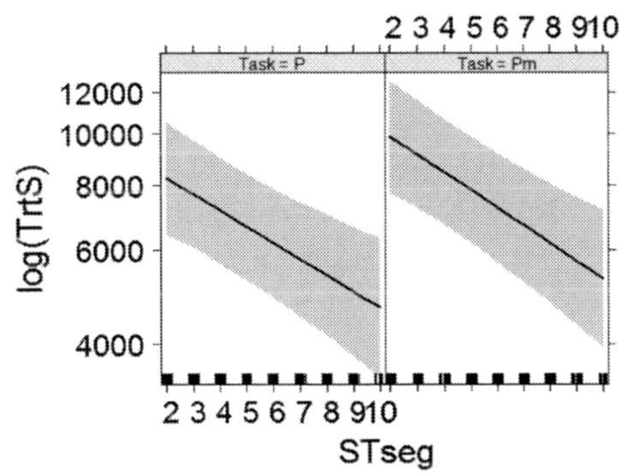

Figure 3: Interaction between Task and *STseg* for total reading time on the ST (*TrtS*)

\+ *TrtT*) spent reading the TT (*Perc_TrtT*). Results were broadly similar (the model with the absolute values was more complex and Task had no significant effect on *TrtT*), but the proportional aspect seemed more informative. The final model for *Perc_TrtT* had the following predictors: the number of deletions (*del*), Task, *STseg* and *Nedit*.

The number of deletions per segment (*del*) had a relatively large, positive and highly significant effect (see Table 5), as did *Nedit*. Task had a small negative effect on *Perc_TrtT*, such that in the mixed mode participants spent slightly less time reading the TT and more time reading the ST - in proportion (see Figure 4). *STseg* had a relatively large, negative and highly significant effect on

Perc_TrtT. The interaction between Task and *Perc_TrtT* was not significant (see Figure 5).

The effect of STseg on *Perc_TrtT* suggests that the cognitively effortful activity of divided attention between languages (source and target) be-

Predictor	β	SE	t	p	
del	0.13	0.03	3.85	1.55E-04	***
Task Pm	-2.13	1.03	-2.06	0.039	*
STseg	2.05	0.25	8.33	3.55E-15	***
Nedit	1.46	0.59	2.47	0.014	*

Table 5: The LMEM for *Perc_TrtT*

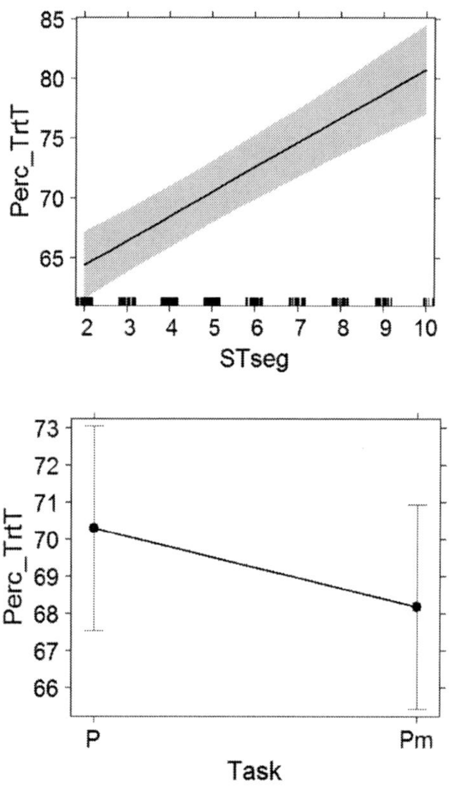

Figure 4: The effect of *Task* and sequential numbering of source segments (*STseg*) on the percentage participants spend reading the TT (*Perc_TrtT*).

comes more centred on the TT (proportionally) as participants progress in the task. This effect is the same in the two modes. Again, what this shows is that the order of the segments in the text and text level coherence more generally plays a negligible role in post-editing - regarding the time spent on the ST and the TT (proportionally). The model for (*Perc_TrtT*) without interaction provided a modest fit (marginal $R^2 = 0.18$, conditional $R^2 = 0.34$).

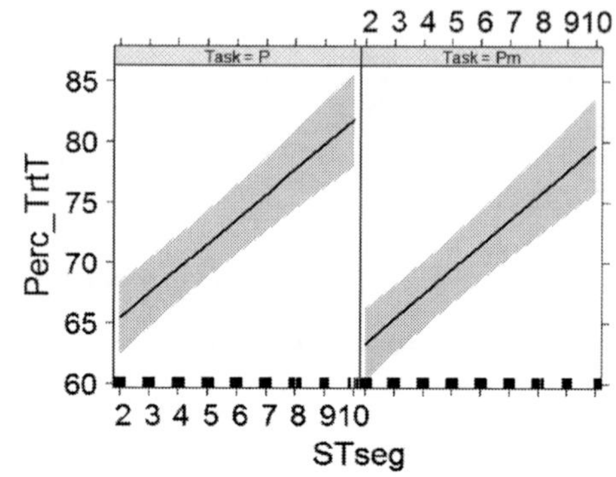

Figure 5:Interaction between Task and *STseg* for (*Perc_TrtT*)

Carl et al. (2016) and similarly Schaeffer et al (2016b) use Activity Units to describe the behaviour during post-editing and from-scratch translation. An Activity Unit slices the data stream of eye movements and keystrokes into 6 types of activity: Either participants read the ST (Type 1), or they read the TT (Type 2), or they produce keystrokes while no eye movements are recorded (Type 4). However, these activities can co-occur: participants may read the ST while (touch) typing (Type 5) or they are reading the TT while typing (Type 6). Finally, if no activity is recorded for more than 2.5 seconds, this is then Type 8. This classification exhaustively slices up the data stream into Activity Units of a certain duration. The duration of Activity Units can be an indicator of how effortful the process is: the longer these activities are, the more effort is required for the particular task such as ST reading (Type 1), TT reading (Type 2) or no recorded activity (Type 8).

The model had the (log transformed) duration of the Activity Unit (*Dur*) as dependent variable and the following predictors Task, Activity Unit Type, the number of fixated words (*PathNmbr*). For Activity Units Type 4 and 8, *PathNmbr* was set to 1, given that these Activity Units do not include any recorded eye movements. And finally the sequential numbering of Activity Units as they occurred (*Id*). *Id* is similar to *STseg* in the previous analyses, in that it can show whether there was a task facilitation effect. The random variable was Participant. In addition, we tested for the interaction between Task and Activity Unit Type and Task and *Id*. The reference level for Activity Unit Type was Type 1.

There was a small, but highly significant effect of Task on the duration of Activity units, such that, in the mixed mode, Activity Units were overall about 100ms shorter than in the coherent mode (see Figure 6). This is not a large effect, but it does indicate that the mixed mode was slightly easier for participants than the coherent mode. *PathNmbr* had an expectedly large, positive and highly significant effect. *Id* also showed a task facilitation effect for the duration of Activity Units - it was relatively large, negative and significant. Neither of the interactions were significant. The model without interactions provided a relatively good fit (marginal $R^2 = 0.46$, conditional $R^2 = 0.47$).

Predictor	β	SE	t	p	
TaskPm	-0.06	0.01	-4.02	5.95E-05	***
PathNmbr	0.11	0.00	73.28	2.00E-16	***
Type2	0.37	0.02	22.38	2.00E-16	***
Type4	0.81	0.17	4.89	1.02E-06	***
Type5	0.04	0.04	0.95	0.344	
Type6	0.57	0.02	26.01	2.00E-16	***
Type8	1.68	0.10	16.43	2.00E-16	***
Id	-0.0004	0.0001	-3.19	0.001	**

Table 6: LMEM for the duration of Activity Units.

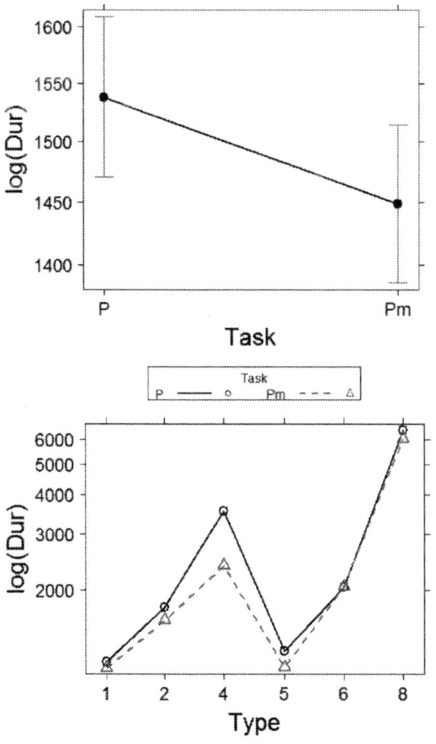

Figure 6:The effect of Task on Activity Unit Duration and the interaction between Activity Unit Type and Task.

In sum, we can say that, in terms of the duration of Activity Units, participants behaved generally in a similar way and if at all, the mixed mode was slightly easier for participants than the coherent mode.

For example, Dragsted (2005) and Alves and Vale (2009) argue that longer stretches of continuous activity are actually indicative of less effortful behaviour. However, in both studies, the definition of a unit occurs on the basis of a pause threshold which defines uninterrupted typing of between 1 and 2 (Dragsted 2005) and 1 and 5 seconds (Alves and Vale 2009). However, the above studies cannot describe what happens during the continuous typing activity, which might actually not be continuous, according to our definition of Activity Units. The effect we report here is much smaller (~100ms) and might well fall within the pauses or typing activities and would thus not be captured by the metrics proposed by the above studies.

6 Discussion

This paper reports from an experiment in which participants post-edited two kinds of texts: in the coherent mode, participants post-edited 2 short texts which were presented as a whole each and in which the order of segments was unaltered. In the mixed mode, participants saw 2 texts which had their segments mixed up and in addition, the order of the segments was jumbled. In the mixed mode, it would have been arguably difficult to generate a text level coherence model, given that the order was jumbled and two texts with rather different topics were jumbled. Surprisingly, this had little or no effect on behaviour.

Maybe most surprisingly, the sequential numbering of segments and of Activity Units had a negative effect on typing duration for both modes. The same was true for the reading times on the ST: participants spent less time on reading the ST the closer they came towards the end of the text - irrespective of whether the segments were presented unaltered or in the mixed mode. Participants spent more time overall reading the ST in the mixed mode than in the coherent, unaltered mode. This was the only instance of an effect which it could be interpreted as a negative consequence of the lack of text level coherence. However, the effect was small (about 1 second per segment). The proportion of time participants read the TT increased as they progressed in the task and this was again true irrespective of whether segments were coherent or jumbled. Activity Units describe minimal types of activity: ST reading, TT reading, TT typing, a combination of the latter and pauses (no recorded eye movements or keystrokes when participants maybe look away from the screen). The duration of Activity Units can be seen as an indicator of cognitive effort - the longer they last, the higher the cognitive effort. Interestingly, participants had overall slightly shorter Activity Units (about 100ms) in the mixed mode. What all these results suggest is that the mixed mode is not detrimental or cognitively more demanding and rather beneficial or equivalent to coherent mode. These results are promising given that presenting segments in an order which differs from how the ST presents the segments makes it possible to (also) present the ST in a different order from the original one, rather than (only) as a coherent text and this, in turn, makes it possible to fully exploit the potential in crowdsourcing by splitting up coherent texts into units that can be translated and edited independently by a large number of translators at the same time.

However, it has to be borne in mind, that the texts used in this study were very small, due to the limitations as dictated by the recording instruments. Professional translators typically translate texts which are much longer, more specialized and with a whole range of tools. A further limitation to our study is that we did not (yet) examine the quality of the TTs before and after post-editing in the two modes. This is a crucial aspect with important ramifications. Despite these limitations it is appropriate to find these findings encouraging - given the sensitivity of the metrics and the broadly positive results: they are positive against the backdrop of arguments brought forward by those who argue against decontextualization, such as Pym (2011) who points out that technology disrupts linearity in texts, because they are segmented and broken into smaller units. The disruption of text's linearity is inherent to both translation memories (TMs) and machine translation (MT) as TMs and MT segments tend to be sentences or sentence-like units. Consequently, working with a text at a sentence level makes it very complicated to provide "an accurate and fluent translation that adheres to the cohesive and contextual norms of the target language, where, for instance, common linguistic devices of cohesion such as anaphora and cataphora typically function at the paragraph and document level" (Doherty, 2016: 954). Although the longer reading times on the source text in the mixed mode may be indicative of the search for coherence in the ST it has to be borne in mind that this effect was very modest in size (~ 1sec per sentence). Serious disruption would have left a much stronger trace in the behavioral data. Participants spent more time on the TT (proportionally) as they progressed in the task (irrespective of mode), i.e., a shift of attention away from the ST to the TT occurred. This suggests a shift from comprehension to production. The opposite would be a clear indicator of disruption. This was not the case.

It remains to be seen what happens if texts are broken down into sub-sentence units and how this affects behavior, quality and productivity. Again, the results presented here are not discouraging.

References

Fabio Alves and José Luiz Gonçalves. 2013. Investigating the conceptual-procedural distinction in the translation process. A relevance-theoretic analysis of micro and macro translation units. *Target: International Journal on Translation Studies*, 25(1), pages 107–124. https://doi.org/10.1075/target.25.1.09alv

Fabio Alves and Daniel Couto Vale. 2009. Probing the unit of translation in time: Aspects of the design and development of a web application for storing, annotating, and querying translation process data. *Across Languages and Cultures: A Multidisciplinary Journal for Translation and Interpreting Studies*, 10(2), pages 251–273. https://doi.org/10.1556/Acr.10.2009.2.5

R. Harald Baayen. 2013. languageR: Data sets and Functions with R. Analyzing Linguistic Data: A Practical Introduction to Statistics. *R package version 1.4.1*

Kamil Bartoń. 2009. MuMIn: Multi-Model Inference. *R Package version 1.15.6.*

Douglas M. Bates, Martin Maechler, Ben Bolker, and Steven Walker. 2014. {lme4}: Linear mixed-effects models using Eigen and S4. *R package version 1.0-6*

Peter F. Brown, J. Cocke, S. Della Pietra, V. Della Pietra, F. Jelinek, R. Mercer, and P. Roossin. 1988. A Statistical Approach to Language Translation. In *Second International Conference on Theoretical and Methodological Issues in Machine Translation of Natural Languages*. pages 71–76.

Michael Carl and Martin Kay. 2011. Gazing and Typing Activities during Translation: A Comparative Study of Translation Units of Professional and Student Translators. *Meta: Translators' Journal* 56 (4), pages 952–75. https://doi.org/10.7202/1011262ar.

Michael Carl. 2012. Translog-II: a Program for Recording User Activity Data for Empirical Reading and Writing Research. In *The Eighth International Conference on Language Resources and Evaluation. 21-27 May 2012, Istanbul, Tyrkiet*. Department of International Language Studies and Computational Linguistics, pages 2–6

Michael Carl, Moritz J. Schaeffer and Srinivas Bangalore. 2016. The CRITT Translation Process Research Database. In Michael Carl, Srinivas Bangalore and Moritz J. Schaeffer (eds.), *New Directions in Empirical Translation Process Research: Exploring the CRITT TPR-DB*. Springer International Publishing, Cham, Heidelberg, New York, Dordrecht, London, pages 13–54.

John C. Catford. 1965. *A Linguistic Theory of Translation: An Essay in Applied Linguistics*, Oxford University Press, Oxford.

Stephen Doherty. 2016. The Impact of Translation Technologies on the Process and Product of Translation. *International Journal of Communication* 10, pages 947–69.

Barbara Dragsted. 2005. Segmentation in Translation: Differences across Levels of Expertise and Difficulty. *Target: International Journal on Translation Studies* 17 (1), pages 49–70. https://doi.org/10.1075/target.17.1.04dra

Barbara Dragsted. 2006: Computer-aided translation as a distributed cognitive task. *Pragmatics & Cognition* 14(2), pages 443-464. https://doi.org/10.1075/pc.14.2.17dra

Barbara Dragsted. 2004. *Segmentation in Translation and Translation Memory Systems. An Empirical Investigation of Cognitive Segmentation and Effects of Integrating a TM System into the Translation Process*. Copenhagen Business School, Copenhagen.

Arnt L. Jakobsen. 2011. Tracking Translators' Keystrokes and Eye Movements with Translog. In Cecilia Alvstad, Adelina Hild, and Elisabet Tiselius (eds.), *Methods and Strategies of Process Research. Integrative Approaches in Translation Studies*. John Benjamins, Amsterdam and Philadelphia, pages 37-55.

Filip Klubička, Antonio M. Toral, and Víctor Sánchez-Cartagenac. 2017. Fine-Grained Human Evaluation of Neural Versus Phrase-Based Machine Translation. *The Prague Bulletin of Mathematical Linguistics*, (108), pages 121–132, https://doi.org/10.1515/pralin-2017-0014

Alexandra Kuznetsova, Rune Haubo Bojesen Christensen and Per Bruun Brockhoff. 2014. lmertest: Tests for Random and Fixed Effects for Linear Mixed Effect Models (lmer Objects of lme4 Package). *R package version 2.0-6*.

Pascual Martínez-Gómez, German Sanchis-Trilles, and Francisco Casacuberta. 2012. Online adaptation strategies for statistical machine translation in post-editing scenarios. *Pattern Recognition*, 45(9), pages 3193–3203. https://doi.org/10.1016/j.patcog.2012.01.011

Abhijit Mishra, Pushpak Bhattacharyya, and Michael Carl. 2013. Automatically predicting sentence translation difficulty. *ACL 2013 - 51st Annual Meeting of the Association for Computational Linguistics, Proceedings of the Conference*, 2, pages 346–351. http://www.aclweb.org/anthology/P13-2062

Daniel Ortiz-Martínez. 2016. Online Learning for Statistical Machine Translation. *Computational Linguistics*, 42(1), pages 121–161. http://dx.doi.org/10.1162/COLI_a_00244

Álvaro Peris, Miguel Domingo, and Francisco Casacuberta. 2016. Interactive neural machine translation. *Computer Speech & Language*. http://dx.doi.org/10.1016/j.csl.2016.12.003

Anthony Pym. 2011. What Technology Does to Translating. *Translation and Interpreting Research* 3 (1), pages 1–9.

R Development Core Team, 2014. *R: A language and environment for statistical computing*, Vienna, Austria.

Lucia Specia. 2011. Exploiting Objective Annotations for Measuring Translation Post-editing Effort. In *Proceedings of the 15th conference of the European Association for Machine Translation*. Leuven, Belgium, pages 73–80.

Antonio M. Toral. 2017. Neural and Phrase-based Machine Translation Quality for Literary Texts. (Book chapter currently under review).

Jean-Paul Vinay and Jean Darbelnet. 1995. *Comparative stylistics of French and English: a methodology for translation*, John Benjamins, Amsterdam and Philadelphia.

Yonghui Wu, Mike Schuster, Zhifeng Chen, Quoc V. Le, Mohammad Norouzi, Wolfgang Macherey, Maxim Krikun, Yuan Cao, Qin Gao, Klaus Macherey, Jeff Klingner, Apurva Shah, Melvin Johnson, Xiaobing Liu, Łukasz Kaiser, Stephan Gouws, Yoshikiyo Kato, Taku Kudo, Hideto Kazawa, Keith Stevens, George Kurian, Nishant Patil, Wei Wang, Cliff Young, Jason Smith, Jason Riesa, Alex Rudnick, Oriol Vinyals, Greg Corrado, Macduff Hughes, Jeffrey Dean. 2016. Google's Neural Machine Translation System: Bridging the Gap between Human and Machine Translation. *ArXiv e-prints*, pages1-23. http://arxiv.org/abs/1609.08144

Comparing Machine Translation and Human Translation: A Case Study

Lars Ahrenberg
Department of Computer and Information Science
Linköping University
lars.ahrenberg@liu.se

Abstract

As machine translation technology improves comparisons to human performance are often made in quite general and exaggerated terms. Thus, it is important to be able to account for differences accurately. This paper reports a simple, descriptive scheme for comparing translations and applies it to two translations of a British opinion article published in March, 2017. One is a human translation (HT) into Swedish, and the other a machine translation (MT). While the comparison is limited to one text, the results are indicative of current limitations in MT.

1 Introduction

In the CFP for this workshop it is claimed that 'Human translation and Machine Translation (MT) aim to solve the same problem'. This is doubtful as translation is not one thing but many, spanning a large space of genres, purposes, and contexts.

The aim of MT research and development is often phrased as 'overcoming language barriers'. To a large extent this aim has been achieved with many systems producing texts of gisting quality for hundreds, perhaps even thousands of language pairs, and (albeit fewer) systems that enable conversations between speakers that do not share a common language. Human translation, however, often has a more ambitious aim, to produce texts that satisfy the linguistic norms of a target culture and are adapted to the assumed knowledge of its readers. To serve this end of the market, MT in combination with human post-editing is increasingly being used (O'Brien et al., 2014). The goals for MT have then also been set higher, to what is often called quality translation, and new 'interactive' and/or 'adaptive' interfaces have been proposed for post-editing (Green, 2015; Vashee, 2017). Thus, when production quality is aimed for, such as in sub-titling or publication of a news item or feature article, human involvement is still a necessity.

Some recent papers claim that MT now is almost 'human-like' or that it 'gets closer to that of average human translators' (Wu et al., 2016). While such claims may be made in the excitement over substantial observed improvements in a MT experiment, they raise the question (again!) of how HT may differ from MT.

Some scholars have argued that MT will never reach the quality of a professional human translator. The limitations are not just temporary, but inherent in the task. These arguments are perhaps most strongly expressed in (Melby with T. Warner, 1995). More recently, but before the breakthrough of NMT, Giammarresi and Lapalme (2016) still consider them valid. As MT can produce human-like translations in restricted domains and is increasingly being included in CAT-tools, they insist that MT is posing a challenge for Translation Studies.

In this paper I report a small case study, a close comparison of a human translation and a machine translation from a state-of-the-art system of the same source text. This is done with two purposes in mind. The first concerns how the differences should be described, what concepts and tools are useful to make such a comparison meaningful and enlightening. The second is to assess the differences between state-of-the-art MT and HT, with the caveat, of course, that one pair of translations cannot claim to be representative of the very large translation universe.

The Proceedings of the First Workshop on Human-Informed Translation and Interpreting Technology (HiT-IT), pages 21–28,
Varna, Bulgaria, Sept 7, 2017

2 MT and Translation Studies

The two fields of MT and Translation Studies (TS) have developed separately for almost as long as they have existed. In the early days of both disciplines, some researchers attempted to account for translation in more or less formal linguistic terms, potentially forming a foundation for automatization, e.g. (Catford, 1965). The 'cultural turn' in TS moved the field away from linguistic detail and further apart from MT. The 1990:ies saw a common interest in empirical data, but while corpora, and parallel corpora in particular, were collected and studied in both fields, they were largely used for different purposes. For example, it seems that the empirical results generated by TS studies on translation universals (Baker, 1993) did not have much effect on MT.

A problem related to this challenge is that MT and TS lack common concepts and terminology. MT prefers to speak in terms of models, whereas TS is more comfortable with concepts such as function and culture. There is a mutual interest in translation quality assessment (TQA), however, and large-scale projects on MT tend to have some participation of TS scholars. For example, one result of the German Verbmobil project is the volume *Machine Translation and Translation Theory*, (Hauenschild and Heizmann, 1997) that contain several studies on human translation and how it can inform MT. It is also true of more recent projects such as QTLaunchPad where evaluation of translation quality was in focus, and CASMACAT where the design of a CAT tool was informed by translation process research (Koehn et al., 2015).

Error analysis is an area of common interest. (O'Brian, 2012) showed that error typologies and weightings were used in all eleven translation companies taking part in her study. It was also shown that some categories occurred in all or the large majority of the taxonomies. She concludes though that error analysis is insufficient and sometimes rightout inappropriate. This is so because it doesn't take a holistic view of the text and its utility and paying too little attention to aspects such as text type, function or user requirements. A number of alternative evaluation models including usability evaluation, ratings of adequacy and fluency, and readability evaluation are propsed.

In the MT context the merits of error analysis is that it can tell developers where the major problems are, and users what to expect. A taxonomy which has been popular in MT is (Vilar et al., 2006). To avoid the necessity of calling in human evaluators every time an error analysis is to be performed there have also been work on automatic error classification (Popović and Burchardt, 2011). While simply counting errors seems less relevant for comparing machine translation to human translation, showing what type of errors occur can be useful. We must recognize then that the categories could vary with purpose.

Another line of research studies the effects of tools and processes on translations. This field is quite underresearched, though see for instance (Jiménez-Crespo, 2009; Lapshinova-Koltunski, 2013; Besacier and Schwartz, 2015) for some relevant studies.

2.1 Comparing Translations

The most common standard for comparing translations is probably quality, a notion that itself requires definition. If we follow the insights of TS, quality cannot be an absolute notion, but must be related to purpose and context. For instance, Mateo (2014), referring to (Nord, 1997) defines it as "appropriateness of a translated text to fulfill a communicative purpose". In the field of Translation Quality Assessment (TQA) the final outcome of such a comparison will then be a judgement of the kind 'Very good', 'Satisfactory', or 'Unacceptable' where at least some of the criteria for goodness refer to functional or pragmatic adequacy (Mateo et al., 2017).

In MT evaluation, which is concerned with system comparisons based on their produced translations, the judgements are more often rankings: 'Better-than' or 'Indistinguishable-from'. One focus has then been on developing metrics whose ratings correlate well with human ratings or rankings. This line of research got a boost by Papineni et al. (2002) and has since been an ongoing endeavour in the MT community, in particular in conjunction with the WMT workshops from 2006 onwards. Most measures developed within MT rely on reference translations and give a kind of measure of similarity to the references.

While judgements such as Good or Unacceptable are of course very relevant in a use context, a comparison of MT and HT may better focus on characteristic properties and capabilities instead. The questions that interest me here are questions such as: What are the characteristics of a machine-translated text as compared to a human translation? What can the human translator do that the MT system cannot (and vice versa)? What actions are needed to make it fit for a purpose?

Many works on translation, especially those that are written for presumtive translators, include a chapter on the options available to a translator, variously called strategies, methods or procedures. A translation procedure is a type of solution to a translation problem. In spite of the term, translation procedures can be used descriptively, to characterize and compare translations, and even to characterize and compare translators, or translation norms. This is the way they will be used here, for comparing human translation and machine translation descriptively. This level of description seems to me to be underused in MT, though see (Fomicheva et al., 2015) for an exception.

With (Newmark, 1988) we may distinguish general or global translation methods, such as semantic vs. communicative translation, that apply to a text as a whole (macro-level) from procedures that apply at the level of words (micro-level), such as shifts or transpositions. In this paper the focus is on the micro-level methods.

3 A Case Study

3.1 The Approach

The analysis covers intrinsic as well as extrinsic or functional properties of the translations. The intrinsic part covers basic statistical facts such as length and type-token ratios, and MT metrics. Its main focus, however, is on translation procedures or the different forms of correspondence that can be found between units. A special consideration is given to differences in word order as these can be established less subjectively than categorizations. The functional part considers purpose and context, but one translation can in principle be evaluated in relation to two or more purposes, i.e., post-editing or gisting.

Catford (1965) introduced the notion of shifts, meaning a procedure that deviates somehow from a plain or literal translation. A large catalogue of translation procedures, or methods, was provided by (Vinay and Darbelnet, 1958) summarized in seven major categories: borrowing, calque, literal translation, transposition, modulation, equivalence, and adaptation. Newmark (1988) provides a larger set. The most detailed taxonomy for translation procedures is probably van Leuven-Zwart (1989) who establishes correspondence on a semantic basis through what she calls architransemes.

A problem with these taxonomies is to apply them in practice. For this reason I will only give counts for coarse top level categories and report more fine-grained procedures only in rough estimates. At the top level we have a binary distinction between Shifts and Unshifted, or literal translations. An unshifted translation is one where only procedures which are obligatory or standard for the target language have been used, and content is judged to be the same. Semantic shifts are as far as possible noted separately from structural shifts.

Shifts are identified at two levels: sentences and clausal units. Relations between units are established on the basis of position and content. At the sentence level position in the linear flow of information is usually sufficient to infer a relation. At the clausal level correspondence must take syntactic relations into account in addition to content. As for content we require only that there is some sort of describable semantic or pragmatic relation.

3.2 The Data

The source text is an opinion article published by the Financial Times on March 17, 2017 entitled *Why I left my liberal London tribe* and written by David Goodhart. It is fairly typical of a British opinion article. Paragraphs are short with only a few sentences, the length of sentences are quite varied, and long sentences tend to be built both syntactically and with insertions, appositions and parataxis. Table 1 (first column) gives an illustration.

The human translation appeared in the June issue of the Swedish magazine *Axess*. It was translated manually with no other computer aids than interactive dictionaries and the web for fact checking. No specific brief had been issued with the assignment. The translation was published with only minor edits but under a different title.

The machine translation was produced by Google Translate in the middle of June, 2017. According to Google's web information, translation from English into Swedish was then using NMT[1].

Even a non-Swedish speaker can observe that the paragraph shown in Table 1 has the same num-

[1] https://cloud.google.com/translate/docs/languages

English source	Swedish MT	Swedish HT
I referred to changing my mind	Jag hänvisade till att ändra mig	Jag refererade till ett byte av uppfattning
as though it were a rational process,	som om det var en rationell process,	som om det vore en rationell process,
in which one audits ones beliefs	där man reviderar sin tro	där man granskar sina åsikter
every few years and decides to	på några år och bestämmer sig för att	med några års mellanrum och beslutar sig för
shift ground on Israel/Palestine	flytta marken mot Israel / Palestina	att ändra ståndpunkt ifråga om Israel och
or the single market.	eller den inre marknaden.	palestinierna eller EU:s inre marknad
But thats not how it works.	Men det är inte hur det fungerar.	Men det är inte så det fungerar.
If, like most educated people,	Om du, som de mest utbildade persone-	Om man, som de flesta välutbildade,
you place a high value on moral and	rna lägger högt värde på moralisk och	sätter stort värde på moralisk och
intellectual coherence, your views	intellektuell sammanhang, har dina	intellektuell samstämmighet brukar ens
tend to fit together into something	åsikter en tendens att passa in i något	åsikter passa in i något som liknar
like an explicable worldview.	som en förklarlig världsutsikt.	en förståelig världsåskådning.
And that usually goes along with	Och det går oftast med	Och med den följer vanligtvis ett
informal membership of a network	informellt medlemskap i ett nätverk	informellt medlemskap i ett nätverk
like-minded people.	av likasinnade människor.	av likasinnade.
Without having to think very hard	Utan att behöva tänka väldigt svårt,	Utan att egentligen behöva fundera på
you know you all broadly favour	känner du dig allihopa	saken vet man att alla på det hela
and oppose the same things.	och motsätter sig samma saker.	taget är för och emot samma saker.

Table 1: A source paragraph and its two translations.

ber of sentences as the source in both translations (there are 5), that the sentences correspond one-to-one and are quite similar in length. The flow of information is also very similar; shorter units than sentences such as clauses and phrases can be aligned monotonously in both translations with few exceptions.

	Source	MT	HT
Paragraphs	30	30	30
Sentences	86	86	95
Word tokens	2555	2415	2603
Characters	13780	13888	15248
Type-token ratio	2.84	2.56	2.58
Mean Sent.length	29.7	28.1	27.4
Avg length diff.	–	2.0	3.2

Table 2: Basic statistics for the three texts. The last line states the average absolute value of length differences at the sentence level.

4 Results

4.1 Basic Statistics

The visual impression of Table 1 indicates that the human translation is longer than the machine translation. This is confirmed when we look at the translations as wholes, the human translation is longer both in terms of number of words and number of characters. In terms of characters the ratio is 1.01 for the MT and 1.11 for the HT. Yet, when the HT is shorter than the source for a given sentence, the difference can be large. The HT also has more sentences, as the human translator has decided to split eight sentences (roughly 9% of all) into two or three shorter ones. Basic statistics for all three texts are shown in Table 2.

MT metrics are especially valuable for comparisons over time. As we only have one machine translation in this study, we limit ourselves to reporting BLEU (Papineni et al., 2002) and TER (Snover et al., 2006). After tokenization and segmentation into clause units of both the MT and the HT translations, using the latter as reference we obtained the results shown in Table 3[2]. Following the analysis of clauses into Shifted and Unshifted (see section 4.4) we also computed these metrics for the two types of segments separately.

Section	BLEU	Bleu(1)	Bleu(2)	TER
Unshifted	42.79	69.0	48.7	0.374
Shifted	16.84	48.2	23.6	0.662
All	23.27	59.6	30.7	0.621

Table 3: BLEU and TER scores for different sections of the MT, using HT as reference.

[2]Values were computed with the multi-bleu.perl script provided with the Moses system, and tercom.7.25, respectively.

4.2 Monotonicity

By monotonicity we mean information on the order of content in the translation as compared to the order of corresponding content in the source text. Both translations are one-to-one as far as paragraphs are concerned. As noted, the HT is not altogether one-to-one at the sentence level, but at the level of clauses, the similarities are greater: the order is the same with the exception that the HT has added one clause.

To get a measure of monotonicity all corresponding word sequences s (from the source text) and t (from the translation) of the form s=a:b and t=Tr(b):Tr(a) are identified. The number of instances per sentence is noted as well as the number of words that are part of such a source sequence. The degree of monotonicity is expressed as a ratio between the total number of affected source words and all words in the text. The results are shown in Table 4.

Word Order changes	MT		HT	
	Sents	Words	Sents	Words
0	36	0	15	0
1	40	125	40	197
2	9	72	22	203
3	1	10	5	52
≥ 4	-	0	4	110
Total	86	207	86	562

Table 4: Number of sentence segments affected by a certain number of word order changes.

A total of 61 changes of word order is observed in the MT, related to 207 words of the source text, or 1.5% of all words. Almost all of them are correct, the large majority of them relates to the V2-property of Swedish main clauses. as in (1), but there are also successful changes producing correct word order in subordinate clauses, as in (2), or a Swedish s-genitive from an English of-genitive as in (3). While the system thus has a high precision in its word order changes, there are also cases where it misses out.

(1) Why do we$_1$ change$_2$ our minds about things?
Varför förändrar$_2$ vi$_1$ vårt sinne om saker?
(2) and feel that for the first time in my life$_1$ I$_2$ ...
och känner att jag$_2$ för första gången i mitt liv$_1$ ...
(3) the core beliefs$_1$ of modern liberalism$_2$
den moderna liberalismens$_2$ kärnföreställningar$_1$

The human translation displays almost twice as many word order changes, 116, and they affect longer phrases and cover longer distances. Still 4.1% is not a very large share and confirms the impression that the information order in the human translation follows the source text closely. The human translator does more than fixing a correct grammar, however, and also improves the style of the text, for instance as regards the placement of insertions, as in (4), and shifts of prominence, as in (5).

(4) I have changed$_1$ my mind, more slowly$_2$, about..
MT: Jag har förändrat$_1$ mig, mer långsamt$_2$, om..
HT: Själv har jag, om än långsammare$_2$, ändrat$_1$ inställning..
(5) Instead I met the intolerance$_1$ of .. for the first time$_2$
MT: Istället mötte jag den intolerans av den moderna vänster$_1$ för första gången$_2$
HT: Istället fick jag för första gången$_2$ möta den moderna v¨nsterns intolerans$_1$

4.3 Purpose-related Analysis

It is obvious, and unsurprising, that the MT does not achieve publication quality. To get a better idea of where the problems are, a profiling was made in terms of the number and types of edits judged to be necessary to give the translation publication quality. Any such analysis is of course subjective, and it has been done by the author, so the exact numbers are not so important. However, the total number and distribution of types are indicative of the character of the translation. A simple taxonomy was used with six types[3]:

- Major edit; substantial edit of garbled output requiring close reading of the source text
- Order edit; a word or phrase needs reordering
- Word edit; a content word or phrase must be replaced to achieve accuracy
- Form edit; a form word must be replaced or a content word changed morphologically
- Char edit; change, addition or deletetion of a single character incl. punctuation marks
- Missing; a source word that should have been translated has not been

The distribution of necessary edits on the different types are shown in Table 4. The most frequent type is 'word edit' which accounts for more than half of all edits. In this group we find words that 'merely' affect style as well as word choices that thwarts the message substantially.

[3]All categories except 'Major edit' have counterparts in the taxonomy of Vilar et al. (2006).

Type of edit	Frequency
Major edit	13
Order edit	24
Word edit	139
Form edit	66
Char edit	13
Missing	21
Total	276

Table 5: Frequencies of different types of required editing operations for the MT (one analyst).

A skilled post-editor could probably perform this many edits in two hours or less. However, there is no guarantee that the edits will give the translation the same quality or reading experience as the human translation. Minimal edits using a segment-oriented interface will probably not achieve that. The style and phrasing of the source would shine through to an extent that could offend some readers of the magazine, although most of the contents may be comprehended without problems, cf. Besacier and Schwartz (2015) on literary text. However, for gisting purposes the MT would be quite adequate.

4.4 Translation Procedures: What the MT System didn't do

While the human translator did not deviate that much in the order of content from the source text, he used a number of other procedures that seem to be beyond the reach of the MT system. Altogether we find more than 50 procedures of this kind in the HT. The most important of these are:

- Sentence splitting. There were eight such splits, including one case of splitting a source sentence into three target sentences. This procedure also comes with the insertion of new material such as a suitable adverb or restoring a subject.
- Shifts of function and/or category. These are numerous; non-finite clauses or NP:s are translated by a finite clause in Swedish, a complete clause is reduced by ellipsis, a relative clause may be rendered by a conjoined clause, adjectival attributes are rendered as relative clauses, an adverb is translated by an adjective or vice versa, and so on.
- Explicitation. Names whose referents cannot be assumed to be known by the readers are explained, e.g. 'Rusell Group universities' receives an explanation in parentheses. Also, at the grammatical level function words such as *och* (and), *som* (relative pronoun), *att* (complementizer 'that') and indefinite articles are inserted more often in the HT than in the MT.
- Modulation = change of point of view. For example, translating 'here' and 'these islands' in the source by 'Storbritannien' (Great Britain).
- Paraphrasing. The semantics is not quite the same but the content is similar enough to preserve the message, e.g. the translation of 'move more confidently through the world' is translated as the terser 'öka ens självsäkerhet' (increase your confidence).

5 Conclusions and Future Work

Differences between machine translations and human translations can be revealed by fairly simple statistical metrics in combination with an analysis based on so-called shifts or translation procedures. In our case, the MT is in many ways, such as length, information flow, and structure more similar to the source than the HT. More importantly, it exhibits a much more restricted repertoir of procedures, and its output is estimated to require about three edits per sentence. Thus, for publishing purposes it is unacceptable without human involvement. Post-editing of the MT output could no doubt produce a readable text, but may not reach the level of a human translation. In future work I hope to be able include post-edited text in the comparison.

Another topic for future research is predicting translation procedures on a par with current shared tasks predicting post-editing effort and translation adequacy.

Acknowledgments

I am indebted to the human translator of the article, Martin Peterson, for information on his assignment and work process, and to the reviewers for pointing out an important flaw in the submitted version.

References

Mona Baker. 1993. Corpus linguistics and translation studies: Implications and applications. In Mona Baker, Gill Francis, and Elena Tognini-Bonelli, editors, *Text and Technology: In Honour of John Sinclair*, John Benjamins, Amsterdam and Philadelphia.

Laurent Besacier and Lane Schwartz. 2015. Automated translation of a literary work: A pilot study. In *Proceedings of the Fourth Workshop on Computational Linguistics for Literature*. Association for Computational Linguistics, Denver, Colorado, USA, pages 114–122. http://www.aclweb.org/anthology/W15-0713.

John C Catford. 1965. *A Linguistic Theory of Translation*. Oxford University Press, London, UK.

Marina Fomicheva, Núria Bel, and Iria da Cunha. 2015. *Neutralizing the Effect of Translation Shifts on Automatic Machine Translation Ev aluation*, Springer International Publishing, pages 596–607. https://doi.org/10.1007/978-3-319-18111-0_45.

Salvatore Giammarresi and Guy Lapalme. 2016. Computer science and translation: Natural languages and machine translation. In Yves Gambier and Luc van Doorslaer, editors, *Border Crossings: Translation Studies and other disciplines*, John Benjamins, Amsterdam/Philadelphia, chapter 8, pages 205–224.

Spence Green. 2015. Beyond post-editing: Advances in interactive translation environments. *ATA Chronicle* Www.atanet.org/chronicle-on-line/...

Christa Hauenschild and Susanne Heizmann. 1997. *Machine Translation and Translation Theory*. De Gruyter.

Miguel A. Jiménez-Crespo. 2009. Conventions in localisation: a corpus study of original vs. translated web texts. *JoSTrans: The Journal of Specialised Translation* 12:79–102.

Philipp Koehn, Vicent Alabau, Michael Carl, Francisco Casacuberta, Mercedes García-Martínez, Jesús González-Rubio, Frank Keller, Daniel Ortiz-Martínez, Germán Sanchis-Trilles, and Ulrich Germann. 2015. Casmacat, final public report. http://www.casmacat.eu/uploads/Deliverables/final-public-report.pdf.

Ekaterina Lapshinova-Koltunski. 2013. Vartra: A comparable corpus for analysis of translation variation. In *Proceedings of the Sixth Workshop on Building and Using Comparable Corpora*. Association for Computational Linguistics, Sofia, Bulgaria, pages 77–86. http://www.aclweb.org/anthology/W13-2510.

Roberto Martínez Mateo. 2014. A deeper look into metrics for translation quality assessment (TQA): A case study. *Miscelánea: A Journal of English and American Studies* 49:73–94.

Roberto Martínez Mateo, Silvia Montero Martínez, and Arsenio Jesús Moya Guijarro. 2017. The modular assessment pack a new approach to translation quality assessment at the directorate general for translation. *Perspectives: Studies in Translation Theory and Practice* 25:18–48. Doi 10.1080/0907676X.2016.1167923.

Alan Melby with T. Warner. 1995. *The Possibility of Language*. John Benjamins, London and New York. https://doi.org/10.1075/btl.14.

Peter Newmark. 1988. *A Textbook of Translation*. Prentice Hall, London and New York.

Christiane Nord. 1997. *Translation as a Purposeful Activity*. St Jerome, Manchester, UK.

Sharon O'Brian. 2012. Towards a dynamic quality evaluation model for translation. *The Journal of Specialized Translation* 17:1.

Sharon O'Brien, Laura Winther Balling, Michael Carl, Michel Simard, and Lucia Specia. 2014. *Post-Editing of Machine Translation: Processes and Applications*. Cambridge Scholars Publishing, Newcastle upon Tyne.

Kishore Papineni, Salim Roukos, Todd Ward, and Wei-Jing Zhu. 2002. Bleu: a method for automatic evaluation of machine translation. In *Proceedings of 40th Annual Meeting of the Association for Computational Linguistics*. Association for Computational Linguistics, Philadelphia, Pennsylvania, USA, pages 311–318. https://doi.org/10.3115/1073083.1073135.

Maja Popović and Aljoscha Burchardt. 2011. From human to automatic error classification for machine translation output. In *Proceedings of the 15th International Conference of the European Association for Machine Translation*. Leuven, Belgium, pages 265–272.

Matthew Snover, Bonnie Dorr, Richard Schwartz, Linnea Micciulla, and John Makhoul. 2006. A study of translation edit rate with targeted human annotation. In *Proceedings of Association for Machine Translation in the Americas*.

Kitty M van Leuven-Zwart. 1989. Translation and original: Similarities and dissimilarities, 1. *Target* 1:2:151–181.

Kirti Vashee. 2017. A closer look at sdl's adaptive mt technology. Http://kv-emptypages.blogspot.se/2017/01/a-closer-look-at-sdls-adaptive-mt.html.

David Vilar, Jia Xu, Luis Fernando D'Haro, and Hermann Ney. 2006. Error analysis of machine translation output. In *LREC06*. Genoa, Italy, pages 697–702.

Jean-Paul Vinay and Jean Darbelnet. 1958. *Stylistique Comparée du Fran cais et de l'Anglais. Méthode de Traduction*. Didier, Paris.

Yonghui Wu, Mike Schuster, Zhifeng Chen, Quoc V. Le, Mohammad Norouzi, Wolfgang Macherey, Maxim Krikun, Yuan Cao, Qin Gao, Klaus Macherey, Jeff Klingner, Apurva Shah, Melvin Johnson, Xiaobing Liu, Lukasz Kaiser, Stephan Gouws, Yoshikiyo Kato, Taku Kudo, Hideto Kazawa, Keith Stevens, George Kurian, Nishant Patil, Wei Wang, Cliff Young, Jason Smith, Jason Riesa, Alex Rudnick, Oriol Vinyals, Greg Corrado, Macduff Hughes, and Jeffrey Dean. 2016. Google's neural machine translation system: Bridging the gap between human and machine translation. *CoRR* abs/1609.08144. Http://arxiv.org/abs/1609.08144.

TransBank: Metadata as the Missing Link between NLP and Traditional Translation Studies

Michael Ustaszewski **Andy Stauder**
University of Innsbruck, Department of Translation Studies
michael.ustaszewski@uibk.ac.at andy.stauder@uibk.ac.at

Abstract

Despite the growing importance of data in translation, there is no data repository that equally meets the requirements of translation industry and academia alike. Therefore, we plan to develop a freely available, multilingual and expandable bank of translations and their source texts aligned at the sentence level. Special emphasis will be placed on the labelling of metadata that precisely describe the relations between translated texts and their originals. This metadata-centric approach gives users the opportunity to compile and download custom corpora on demand. Such a general-purpose data repository may help to bridge the gap between translation theory and the language industry, including translation technology providers and NLP.

1 Introduction

The breakthroughs in machine learning of the past years have made statistical approaches the dominant paradigm in Natural Language Processing (NLP) in general and in Machine Translation (MT) in particular. As a consequence, translation data such as parallel corpora, translation memories (TM) and postediting data have become of utmost importance to the increasingly (semi-)automated translation industry. The "datafication of translation" (Wang, 2015; van der Meer, 2016) observed in the industry is no exception in the era of big data.

Driven by the irreversible trend towards translation automation and the resulting demand for more and more data, several industry-led projects for the large-scale collection of translation data have been launched (see section 2.1). These projects mainly aim to boost productivity in the language industry and are therefore oriented towards the needs of language service providers (LSPs), translation technology developers and, to a lesser extent, of translators. While such data repositories are without doubt useful not only for the translation industry but also for a range of lines of research in Translation Studies (TS), we believe that they do not fully accommodate the needs of the latter. The reason for this is that although they cover a large variety of language pairs, subject domains and text types, they pay insufficient attention to metadata about the included texts and text segments. After all, the object of study in TS is not limited to translation products but extends to translation processes and the linguistic, cognitive, socio-cultural, socio-economic and technological factors that influence translation. Translation data without metadata is only of limited use for research into the complex nature of translation because metadata describe how, when and under what circumstances a given text has been produced. For the training of NLP systems and for productivity gains in the translation industry, these questions are less of a concern, at least for the present.

In the academic discipline of TS, the trend towards data-driven methods is far less pronounced than in the translation industry and among translation technology providers. A bibliometric analysis has revealed that corpus-based research is gaining momentum in TS but still noticeably trails behind the most popular lines of research (Zanettin et al., 2015). To avoid losing relevance to the translation industry and translation technology providers, TS needs to continue adopting and developing more rigorous, empirically sound and objective methods of scientific inquiry. Furthermore, as Way and Hearne (2011) highlighted, in order to advance MT, we need to make explicit the phenomena that occur in real translated data and model these phenomena more effectively in a joint effort of MT developers, translators and translation scholars. A closer collaboration between these major stakeholders in translation would be a big step towards narrowing the yawning and growing gap between

The Proceedings of the First Workshop on Human-Informed Translation and Interpreting Technology (HiT-IT), pages 29–35,
Varna, Bulgaria, Sept 7, 2017

translation theory and translation practice, identified i.a. by Sun (2014), and to eventually provide innovative solutions to unresolved problems in MT. For this endeavor to be successful, the availability of high-quality, labelled real-world translation data is paramount.

Against this background, we aim to develop a novel resource that equally meets the requirements of all translation stakeholders, be it translation scholars, translation technology developers, LSPs, translators, translation trainers and trainees, or researchers from neighboring disciplines interested in translation and translated language. The key to such a general-purpose collection of translation data is a precise and comprehensive set of metadata labels that help capture the relation between translated texts and their originals, including the circumstances under which the translations were produced. Translated target texts (TTs) and their source texts (STs) will be stored in a freely available, open-ended and growing bank of translation data – hence the project name TransBank. The dynamic and metadata-centric approach is expected to combine the advantages of pre-existing data collections and to give users the opportunity to compile and download translational corpora on demand, tailored to the requirements of specific research questions or applications.

In this article, which is mainly meant to be a vision paper, we aim to outline the goals, concept, and planned architecture of TransBank, whose development will start in September, 2017.

2 Related Work

Given the vast amount of bi- and multilingual corpora, an overview of related work is necessarily selective and incomplete.[1] For the sake of simplicity, existing repositories can be grouped into resources oriented mainly towards the language industry and/or NLP one the one hand, and towards academia on the other. The following two subsections summarize, in accordance with this distinction, several selected resources that share some but not all features with TransBank.

2.1 Industry- and NLP-Oriented Resources

The TAUS Data Cloud[2] is the largest industry-shared TM repository, exceeding 79 billion words in more than 2,200 language pairs. Its main aim is to boost the language service sector, which is why it focuses mainly on economically relevant aspects of the industry. It is mainly used to train MT systems, in both industry and academia. Users can download data if they have enough credits, which can be either bought or earned by uploading one's own translation data. Data is searchable on the basis of a relatively small set of metadata labels: source and target language, domain, content type, data owner, and data provider.

MyMemory[3], operated by the LSP *Translated*, also claims to be the world's largest TM. It comprises the TMs of the European Union and United Nations as well as data retrieved from multilingual websites. Its main target groups are, again, the language industry, NLP developers and translators. The download of TMs is free of charge. The search options based on metadata are limited to language pairs and subject domains.

The European Parliament Proceedings Parallel Corpus (EuroParl, Koehn, 2005) has been highly influential in statistical MT due to its large size, multilingual and sentence-aligned architecture. However, it includes a rather limited range of subject domains and text types. Metadata are very scarce (languages and language directions, speaker turns), which limits its usefulness for many potential research questions outside NLP.

The European Commission made a number of its large multilingual TMs and corpora from the domains of politics, law and economy freely available[4]. These resources are often used to train MT systems and to feed TMs in the industry. They, too, provide rather scarce metadata.

Finally, OPUS (Tiedemann, 2012) is a freely available, growing collection of pre-existing, automatically enriched (e.g. POS-tagged) corpora and TMs retrieved from the web. Its main assets are size, the large number of language pairs, textual diversity in terms of subject domains and text types, variation of translation modes (written translation, localization, and subtitles), as well as its open-ended nature. On the downside, metadata are scarce: it provides varying but small label sets depending on the respective processed corpus that is accessed through the OPUS interface, e.g. the EuroParl corpus. Due to its size, variation and free availability, it has proved useful for NLP and MT systems.

[1] For a more comprehensive yet somewhat outdated corpus survey, see Xiao (2008).

[2] https://www.taus.net/data/taus-data-cloud

[3] http://mymemory.translated.net

[4] https://ec.europa.eu/jrc/en/language-technologies

2.2 Academia-Oriented Resources

The Dutch Parallel Corpus (Macken et al., 2011) is a balanced, high-quality and non-growing parallel corpus covering Dutch, English and French, with translations both from and into Dutch. Its advantages are textual variation (19 different types), translational variation (human translation, translation using TMs, postediting and relay translation), as well as variation of ST context. Rich metadata, such as author, text type, publishing information, domain, translation mode, etc., are available.

The Translational English Corpus[5] comprises several sub-corpora of different textual genres and provides a wealth of metadata about texts' extralinguistic parameters, including data about the translators who produced the texts. Contrary to the other resources outlined here, this corpus is not a parallel but a monolingual comparable one, contrasting original English with translated English. It has been influential in TS, especially for research into translationese and stylistic variation.

The MeLLANGE Learner Translator Corpus[6] is a notable representative of multilingual learner corpora and therefore does not include professional translations, but translations produced by translators-in-training. While its size is comparatively small, it provides a wealth of translation-specific metadata on various levels, including information about translators' profiles and the translation processes (e.g. time spent and type of translation aids used). It is most suitable for the study of didactic aspects of translation and of translation quality.

Finally, the Human Language Project (Abney and Bird, 2010) attempted to build a universal corpus of all of the world's languages for the study of language universals and for language documentation. Although not a translation corpus as such, it is of interest to TransBank due to its aim to include as many languages as possible.

From the short survey, it should have become obvious that the reviewed resources differ considerably from each other and that they address different target groups. To a certain extent, their design and architecture reflects the underlying research question or application they have been developed for. In other words, there is no universal, general-purpose repository of translation data suitable for a maximally broad variety of translation-related problems. We believe that the availability of such a resource may both spur data-driven research in TS and foster the collaboration between different stakeholders in translation. To this aim, we plan to develop TransBank as outlined in the following section.

3 TransBank

TransBank is conceived as a large, multilingual, open and expandable collection of translated texts and their originals aligned at sentence level. The core feature is the ability to compile and download parallel sub-corpora on demand, tailored to the requirements regarding specific questions of translation research or translation technology development. TransBank is a meta-corpus in a double sense: firstly, it is a corpus of corpora, and, secondly it provides a rich description of metadata. The analogy is that of a library: When scientists try to answer research questions, they first query the library catalogue to find relevant literature. The library does not provide the answers, but the materials that may contain the answers. In the same way, scientists will be able to turn to TransBank in search of data that may help them to solve their translation-related problems. Note, however, that TransBank will *not* be a metasearch engine, because it will contain the data itself rather than searching for data in third-party resources. TransBank thus closely resembles so-called biobanks, which store biological specimens (e.g. tissue samples) for future use in biomedical research.

The goals of TransBank can be summarized as follows: First, to build an open-ended collection of translations and their STs, aligned at the sentence level. Second, to define a finite set of metadata labels that help capture the distinctive features of translations as highly intertextual language material. Third, to label the data in the bank using the defined metadata labels. And, fourth, to make the data freely available in a highly user-friendly and interoperable form.

The universality and usefulness of TransBank for both academia and the industry is to be ensured by means of the following features:

- **Size**: No size limits are to be set, which implies that the collection will not be a balanced one.
- **Open-endedness**: The collection will grow dynamically, which allows diachronic studies of language and translation over time.

[5] http://www.alc.manchester.ac.uk/translation-and-intercultural-studies/research/projects/translational-english-corpus-tec/

[6] http://mellange.eila.jussieu.fr/public_doc.en.shtml

- **"Omnilinguality"**: The collection will not be limited to certain language pairs; on the contrary, the more languages, the more useful the resource will become.
- **Authenticity:** The project is empirical, yet not experimental in nature: it does not aim to include any translations specially made for the project, but to collect real-world translation data only.
- **Textual variation** in terms of genre, subject domains and text types.
- **Translational variation** in terms of different modes of translation (specialized translation, literary translation, localization, subtitling, relay translation, retranslation, post-edited texts, etc.). Any text that on whatever grounds is representative of the population of translations in the broadest sense may be included into the collection. A yet-to-be-developed definition will help to deal with borderline cases on theoretical grounds.
- **Translator Variation**: Not only translations carried out by professionals are to be included, but also trainee translators' works (as in the case of learner corpora) or amateur translations (as in the case of crowdsourced translation or fansubbing corpora, e.g. OpenSubtitles[7]).
- **Alignment** of texts at sentence level.
- **Metadata labelling** using a fine-grained and objectivity-oriented label set.
- **Download** of TMX and plain text files.
- **High quality** ensured by semi-automatic data collection and manual processing.
- **User-Friendliness** of search interface.
- **Free availability** under CC license.

3.1 Data Collection

As TransBank is only in its pre-project stage, only a few thousand words of test data for the DE-EN language direction have been collected. However, the following is to outline the collection principles to be used during the actual project.

The platform is to impose no restrictions regarding language pairs and directions, genres, text types, subject domains, translator experience and status, time of production, etc. The only two criteria for selection are that texts must be translations paired with their respective originals, and that texts are legally unproblematic in terms of copyright laws and data privacy. Data Selection will be guided by a data harvesting plan that comprises two components: the retrospective collection of legacy data on the one hand and the prospective collection of new data on the other. The retrospective collection consists in enriching existing resources (hence legacy data) with metadata, whereas the prospective collection aims to source and label new data not yet included in any repository. Collecting new data presupposes that the respective translators or LSPs are prepared to provide data and metadata corresponding to our label set already from the start. In this regard, our prospective data collection resembles the TAUS Data Cloud or Translated's MyMemory, where users contribute their own data, with the important difference that submitted data will undergo metadata labelling prior to inclusion. The prospective approach is expected to yield significant quantities of non-literary texts, i.e. text types that constitute the bulk the translation industry's output but that are often underrepresented in translational corpora. As a matter of fact, the focus on literary translation in TS is deemed to be a major factor contributing to the theory-practice gap (Sun 2014); therefore we hope that TransBank may help to narrow the gap. The prospective collection of data will require a community effort between the TransBank project and partners from academia and industry. An incentive for LSPs, especially small ones, is that they will receive manually checked sentence alignment for the data they provide, free of cost, which they can then ingest into their CAT systems.

3.2 Metadata

At this point, the question why metadata is crucial to the TransBank project remains to be answered. The answer has a theoretical and a practical perspective.

At the theoretical end, one must recall the difference between data and information: data is only the body of recorded facts, whereas information refers to the patterns that underlie these facts and that are a prerequisite to gain knowledge about something. In order to identify patterns, in turn, one must be able to group a series of observed facts according to some shared ontological charac-

[7] www.opensubtitles.org

teristics. This is especially true of corpora, which consist of samples of language in use (*parole*) taken out of their natural communicative context. Metadata help to restore that context (Burnard, 2005) and to form subgroups of language samples by relating them to the population they were originally taken from.

On the practical end, sample grouping according to some shared features corresponds to the compilation of sub-corpora tailored to certain previously specified criteria, for example for the training of domain-specific MT systems from the perspective of NLP, for the compilation of domain-specific TMs in the translation industry, or for the gathering of research data to investigate a specific translation-related problem from the perspective of TS. No less important, fine-grained metadata allows to filter data and thus to reduce noise in subsamples, which is very important in the case of very large data collections.

TransBank metadata are to include all major aspects relevant to the production of the translation, such as target language, text type, subject domain, intended use, translator experience and education, use of translation aids, time of production etc. What is decidedly not going to be labelled is translation quality, as this is an issue that has still not been resolved by the scientific community: the translation bank would provide a valuable, re-usable resource for tackling this research question. A separate subset of the labels will have to be defined for STs as they, too, have a number of key features relevant to translation, e.g. source language, year, place and channel of publication, genre and text type, intended audience, if they are translations themselves (resulting in intermediary translation), and so forth. Summing up, the set of metadata labels will provide a precise and generally valid tool to describe the intertextual relation between STs and TTs.

As for the collection of the metadata, these will in part be provided by text donors and reviewed/completed by trained project staff, researching missing entries as well as possible. In this regard, cooperation by data donors is again expected to be improved by the added value provided to them in the form of cost-free sentence alignment.

3.3 Data Storage and Access

Data Storage will be provided in the form of TMX files for the aligned text and METS as a container format for metadata. The web-based search and presentation platform is to provide output options for the download of the texts, which can be generated via XSLT from the above XML formats: plain text of STs and TTs, and TEI compliant XML-files for those who want to label data within the texts as well, as opposed to our metadata about the texts. The TMX/METS files will be available for download as well.

The platform will allow for faceted search operations, which can be used for downloading specific sub-corpora. This means that search parameters can be combined instead of only used in a mutually exclusive manner, as is the case with fixed, separate (sub-)corpora or hierarchically labelled data. One of the most common use cases of faceted search is the narrowing of search results in online-shopping: e-commerce platforms allow users to tick categories, i.e. search facets, such as *manufacturer*, *price range*, *user rating*, *shipment options*, etc. In the discussed meta-corpus, the combination is not only one of various labels for one group of texts, but for two: users have to choose a combination of metadata labels for the STs on the one hand and for the pertinent TTs on the other. The resulting search mask is therefore two-sided. Table 1 shows an example of a query to compile a parallel Bulgarian-English corpus of fictional texts published in Bulgaria between 1995 and 2017 and translated by female translators into their native language English.

Source texts (included in download **[yes]** / [no])	Target texts (included in download **[yes]** / [no])
[language (Bulgarian)] [published from (1995) to (2017)] [published in (Bulgaria)] [genre (fictional)]	[language (English)] [translator (female)] [translation into (native language)]

Table 1: Example query in two-sided mask.

As can be seen in Table 1, users can also choose if STs, TTs or both are to be included in the download, i.e., corpora consisting of only STs or only TTs are an option, too, both of which not necessarily monolingual. This makes it possible to generate comparable corpora as well, e.g. by searching for all original texts from a certain subject domain in various languages, without considering the translations included in the bank. The search engine to be used is Elasticsearch[8].

[8] https://www.elastic.co/products/elasticsearch

4 Expected Outcomes

While sharing a number of features with each of the resources reviewed in section 2, the combination of features, together with a new way of accessing translation data via the envisaged web-platform for faceted search, is expected to provide a genuinely new repository of translation data. The main innovative feature is the ability to compile and download parallel or comparable sub-corpora on demand, tailored to the requirements of specific translation-related problems. This may be beneficial to all stakeholders in translation.

From the perspective of TS, a universal translation repository may promote data-driven research. This, in turn, may increase objectivity, validity and reliability of research and eventually make TS more compliant with the scientific method – a desideratum well in line with the growing awareness of the importance of more rigorous research in TS (Künzli, 2013). The range of possible studies using TransBank data is virtually limitless. Studies may include, for example, diachronic issues such as translation-induced language change; the impact of translation tools on linguistic features of written text; contrastive questions regarding differences between text-type norms and conventions across languages; explorations of the characteristics of crowdsourced translation; or cognitive research interests in connection with the differences between texts produced by trainees and experienced practitioners. It is important to note at this juncture that TransBank does not itself aim to answer such questions, but to provide a resource that facilitates such studies. Therefore, the planned first version does not include any tools aimed at complex analyses of translation material (e.g. collocations), only for searching and compiling it.

From the perspective of NLP and translation technology providers, the openness and targeted high quality of sentence-aligned translation data is expected to make the repository useful for the training and testing of new systems. The focus on metadata will facilitate the collection of custom domain-specific data. The dynamic and open-ended nature will yield a sufficiently large data quantity for big data approaches.

From the perspective of the industry, it is again the availability of domain-specific TMs and training data for MT what makes the repository interesting to LSPs as well as individual translators.

Finally, from the perspective of translator training, the analysis of authentic data rather than made-up examples has great didactic potential, especially when contrasting professional with non-professional translations. Similarly, the use of TransBank as a learner corpus to find recurrent translation errors in groups of trainee translators may help to improve translator training.

On a more general level, the approach to metadata labelling applied to TransBank has the potential of becoming a generally valid translation-specific metadata standard in academia and the industry. The importance of standardization is not to be underestimated in view of the ever increasing amounts of translation data being produced and demanded in the digital era.

5 Conclusion

The main problem to be addressed by the TransBank project is a lack of translation data that may be used to make explicit real-world translation phenomena and provide sound theoretical models capable of explaining them. This would benefit not only TS as a discipline in the tradition of the humanities, but the language industry, including translation technology providers and NLP developers, as well. TransBank is therefore conceived as a universal one-stop repository to serve the needs of all stakeholders in translation.

In summary, what we are aiming to provide is a re-usable, open, sustainable and dynamic collection of real-world translation data covering a large variety of languages, genres, subject domains, text types, translation modes, translator profiles and text production settings. Users will be able to download parallel and/or comparable corpora on demand, tailored to their specific translation-related problems. The key to such a customizable flexibility is a precise set of metadata labels that capture the relation between translated texts and their originals, including the circumstances under which the translations were produced.

Given its universal nature, TransBank may promote the collaboration between various interest groups in translation. It is therefore a link between the translation industry, NLP and academia in a data-centric world.

Acknowledgments

TransBank is funded by the *go!digital 2.0* program of the Austrian Academy of Sciences. We also thank the three anonymous reviewers for their helpful comments.

References

Steven Abney and Steven Bird. 2010. The human language project: building a Universal Corpus of the world's languages. In *Proceedings of the 48th Annual Meeting of the Association for Computational Linguistics (ACL '10)*. Association for Computational Linguistics, Stroudsburg, PA, USA, 88-97. http://aclanthology.coli.uni-saarland.de/pdf/P/P10/P10-1010.pdf.

Lou Burnard. 2005. Metadata for Corpus Work. In Martin Wynne, editor, *Developing Linguistic Corpora: A Guide to Good Practice*. Oxbow Books, Oxford, pages 30-46.

Philipp Koehn. 2005. Europarl: A Parallel Corpus for Statistical Machine Translation. In *Proceedings of the Tenth Machine Translation Summit*, pages 79-86.

Alexander Künzli. 2013. Empirical approaches. In Yves Gambier and Luc van Doorslaer, editors, *Handbook of Translation Studies. Volume 4*. John Benjamins, Amsterdam, pages 53-58.

Lieve Macken, Orphée De Clercq and Hans Paulussen. 2011. Dutch Parallel Corpus: A Balanced Copyright-Cleared Parallel Corpus. *Meta*, 56(2):374-390. http://dx.doi.org/10.7202/1006182ar.

Sanjun Sun. 2014. Rethinking translation studies. *Translation Spaces*, 3:167-191. dx.doi.org/10.1075/ts.3.08sun.

Jörg Tiedemann. 2012. Parallel Data, Tools and Interfaces in OPUS. In *Proceedings of the 8th International Conference on Language Resources and Evaluation (LREC 2012)*, pages. 2214-2218. http://www.lrec-conf.org/proceedings/lrec2012/pdf/463_Paper.pdf.

Jaap van der Meer. 2016. Datafication of Translation. In *TAUS Blog*. www.taus.net/blog/datafication-of-translation.

Peng Wang. 2015. Datafication of Translation. In *Keynotes 2015. A Review of TAUS October Events*. TAUS Signature Editions, Amsterdam, pages 11-14. www.taus.net/think-tank/reports/event-reports/keynotes-2015.

Andy Way and Mary Hearne. 2011. On the Role of Translations in State-of-the-Art Statistical Machine Translation. *Language and Linguistics Compass*, 5:227-248.

Richard Z. Xiao. 2008. Well-known and influential corpora. In Anke Lüdeling and Merja Kytö, editors, *Corpus Linguistics: An International Handbook. Volume 1*. Mouton de Gruyter, Berlin, pages 383-457.

Federico Zanettin, Gabriela Saldanha and Sue-Ann Harding. 2015. Sketching landscapes in translation studies: A bibliographic study. *Perspectives*, 23(2):161-182. dx.doi.org/10.1080/0907676X.2015.1010551.

Interpreting Strategies Annotation in the WAW Corpus

Irina Temnikova[1], Ahmed Abdelali[1], Samy Hedaya[2], Stephan Vogel[1], and Aishah Al Daher[2]

[1]Qatar Computing Research Institute, HBKU, Doha, Qatar
[2]Translation and Interpreting Institute, HBKU, Doha, Qatar
[1,2]{itemnikova,aabdelali,shedaya,svogel,aaldaher}@hbku.edu.qa

Abstract

With the aim to teach our automatic speech-to-text translation system human interpreting strategies, our first step is to identify which interpreting strategies are most often used in the language pair of our interest (English-Arabic). In this article we run an automatic analysis of a corpus of parallel speeches and their human interpretations, and provide the results of manually annotating the human interpreting strategies in a sample of the corpus. We give a glimpse of the corpus, whose value surpasses the fact that it contains a high number of scientific speeches with their interpretations from English into Arabic, as it also provides rich information about the interpreters. We also discuss the ***difficulties***, which we encountered on our way, as well as our ***solutions*** to them: our methodology for manual re-segmentation and alignment of parallel segments, the choice of annotation tool, and the annotation procedure. Our annotation findings explain the previously extracted specific statistical features of the interpreted corpus (compared with a translation one) as well as the quality of interpretation provided by different interpreters.

1 Introduction

As manual translation is slow, often repetitive, and requires a lot of cognitive efforts and the use of additional resources (e.g. dictionaries, encyclopedias, etc.), part of it is now done automatically. Thanks to these recent advances in technology, translation is done in a much faster and sometimes more accurate way. One of the automatic translation tools, Machine Translation (MT) (Hutchins and Somers, 1992) in its present state is used (with pre- and post-editing) in many companies and public institutions.

Despite recent improvements in MT (e.g. Neural MT), automatic MT systems still lack the precision and fluency of human translators and interpreters (Shimizu et al., 2013), and are often criticized because of that. Due to this, we want to teach our in-house speech-to-text (S2T) machine translation system (Dalvi et al., 2017) the techniques human interpreters use.

Human interpreters run several heavy-load processes in parallel (e.g. processing speaker's input, translating and pronouncing the previously heard input, monitoring their own speech, and correcting previous errors (Kroll and De Groot, 2009). To overcome time and brain processing limitations, and the inability to go back and correct their own output, they use many strategies (Kroll and De Groot, 2009; Al-Khanji et al., 2000; Liontou, 1996).

Before learning which human interpreting strategies can improve our S2T system, we run a corpus analysis.

We use a corpus of transcripts of conference speeches, their simultaneous interpretations (performed by professional interpreters), and their manual translations. We first extract surface features (Section 4). Next, we manually annotate coarse-grained interpreting strategies (Section 6) in a sample of the corpus.

The rest of this article is structured as follows: Section 2 summarizes the related work; Section 3 presents our WAW corpus, Section 4 presents some corpus statistics; Section 5 describes the corpus segmentation and alignment methods; Section 6 provides the annotation procedure. Section 7 presents the annotation results, and Section 8 is the Conclusion.

The Proceedings of the First Workshop on Human-Informed Translation and Interpreting Technology (HiT-IT), pages 36–43,
Varna, Bulgaria, Sept 7, 2017

2 Related Work

Before being able to identify which Interpreters' Strategies (IS) could benefit our speech-to-text translation system, we first studied the **existing work on Interpreting Strategies in Interpreting Studies**.

There is substantial research in this area (especially corpus-based), e.g. (Roderick, 2002; Shlesinger, 1998; Bartłomiejczyk, 2006; Liontou, 2012; Hu, 2016; Wang, 2012; Bendazzoli and Sandrelli, 2009; Lederer, 1978; Al-Khanji et al., 2000; Liontou, 1996; Tohyama and Matsubara, 2006).

The research outlines a number of strategies interpreters use in order to alleviate the working memory overload and time shortage. Although different researchers divide and classify them differently, the strategies can be roughly classified (Kalina, 1998; Al-Khanji et al., 2000) into:

1. **Comprehension strategies** (e.g. *preparation, gathering of topic information, terminology check-up, anticipation, chunking* a.k.a. *segmentation* or *salami-technique*),
2. **Target-text production strategies** (e.g. source-text conditioned strategies, such as *transcoding*; target-text conditioned strategies, such as *ear-voice span manipulation, expansion*, and compression or simplification techniques – such as: *passivization* and *omission*; *self-correction, decision for no-self-correction*),
3. **Other strategies** (e.g. buying time by pronouncing generic utterances or delaying the response, *self-monitoring*),
4. **Compensatory strategies** (e.g. *approximation, filtering, omissions, substitutions*).

Some researchers investigate language-pair-specific strategies, e.g. Tohyama and Matsubara (2006); Liontou (1996).

MT researchers' interest on applying interpreters skills to MT was driven by the advances in automatic Speech Translation (ST). Languages with different syntax and word order are a problem for real time and simultaneous ST. Paulik and Waibel (2009) exploited the availability of parallel recordings to leverage on the scarcity of parallel text between English and Spanish. In this way they achieved better than expected performance in MT. Their findings were a motivation to exploit the data produced by interpreters in order to further improve MT. Shimizu et al. (2013) used information learned from simultaneous interpretation data to improve their MT system between Japanese and English, as these two languages have very different grammatical structure and word order. Results showed that emulating the simultaneous interpreters style helped both to improve the accuracy of the system while minimizing the delay before translation generation. Sridhar et al. (2013) made a corpus analysis for simultaneity, hesitations, compression, the lag between source language and target language words, and the use of deixis. He et al. (2016) also made corpus analysis to discover which strategies interpreters use and analysed segmentation, passivization, generalisation, and summarization. Finally, Hauenschild and Heizmann (1997) are a collection of papers from the time of VerbMobil, which contains MT papers inspired by translation and interpreting, as well as translation and interpreting papers, which contribute to MT.

3 The WAW Corpus

The corpus we use in our experiment is a corpus of recordings of speeches/lectures from conferences held in Doha, Qatar. The **WAW** corpus contains 521 recorded sessions (127h 10min 38sec) collected during talks at **WISE** 2013 (World Innovation Summit for Education)[1], **ARC**'14 (Qatar Foundation's Annual Research Conference, a general conference on many topics)[2], and **WISH** 2014 (World Innovation Summit for Health)[3] research conferences in Doha, Qatar. Both speeches in English as a source language (subsequently translated into Modern Standard Arabic), and in Arabic as a source language (subsequently translated into English) are present. From the ethical point of view, all conference speakers signed a release form to transfer the ownership to the conferences organisers (Qatar Foundation). The names of interpreters are not published.

The speeches contained in the corpus have been:

1. **Interpreted by professional interpreters** hired by the conference organisers.
2. **Transcribed by professional transcribers,**

[1]http://www.wise-qatar.org/2013-summit-reinventing-education-life.

[2]http://marhaba.qa/qatar-foundations-annual-research-conference-arc14-calls-on-local-research-expertise/.

[3]http://www.wish-qatar.org.

according to our guidelines.

3. **Translated by professional translators.** The transcripts of both the original speakers and their interpretations have been translated by professional translators, according to our guidelines, into Arabic (if the original language was English) or into English (if the original language was Arabic).

95% of the source/original speeches were in English.

Figure 1 shows the resulting corpus composition. For each speech, we have two audios and four corresponding texts (Original transcript, Interpretation transcript, translation of the source language original transcript and the translation for the target language interpretation transcript).

Out of the 521 recorded sessions, 266 sessions (63h 48min 05sec) contain the complete pack of translations of both source speech transcripts and interpreted target language transcripts.

In total, there were 12 interpreters. According to information from the conference organisers, most of the interpreters were experienced, but we do not have any details about their level of proficiency or areas of expertise.

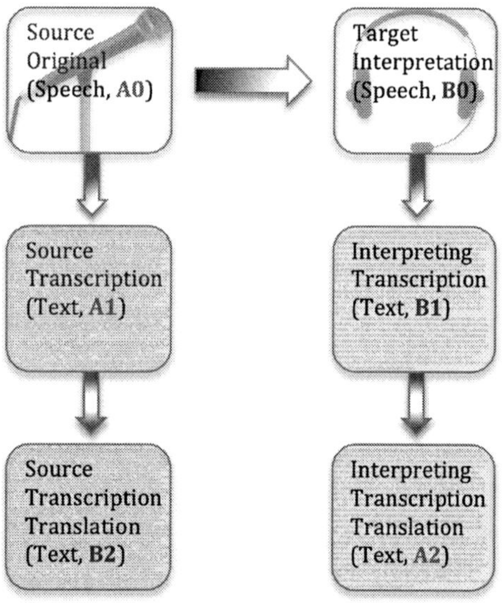

Figure 1: WAW Corpus Composition.

Out of this data, we have mainly used the original speakers' and interpreters' transcripts.

4 WAW Corpus' Assessment

Table 1 shows WAW's size in number of files, time recorded, number of lines/segments, and number of words.

The different number of *Segments* between the Arabic transcripts and the English ones was due to the fact that the initial segmentations of the original speakers' audios and interpreters' audios, as received by the companies were done independently by different transcribers.

Figure 2 shows the different segmentation of the same original speech transcript and its interpretation (both audios with a length of around 50 sec).

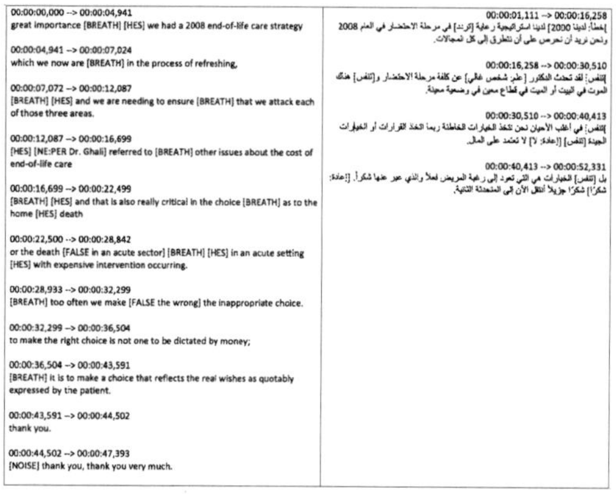

00:00:00,000 --> 00:00:04,941 great importance [BREATH] [HES] we had a 2008 end-of-life care strategy 00:00:04,941 --> 00:00:07,024 which we now are [BREATH] in the process of refreshing, 00:00:07,072 --> 00:00:12,087 [BREATH] [HES] and we are needing to ensure [BREATH] that we attack each of those three areas. 00:00:12,087 --> 00:00:16,699 [HES] [NE:PER Dr. Ghali] referred to [BREATH] other issues about the cost of end-of-life care 00:00:16,699 --> 00:00:22,499 [BREATH] [HES] and that is also really critical in the choice [BREATH] as to the home [HES] death 00:00:22,500 --> 00:00:28,842 or the death [FALSE in an acute sector] [BREATH] [HES] in an acute setting [HES] with expensive intervention occurring. 00:00:28,933 --> 00:00:32,299 [BREATH] too often we make [FALSE the wrong] the inappropriate choice. 00:00:32,299 --> 00:00:36,504 to make the right choice is not one to be dictated by money; 00:00:36,504 --> 00:00:43,591 [BREATH] it is to make a choice that reflects the real wishes as quotably expressed by the patient. 00:00:43,591 --> 00:00:44,502 thank you. 00:00:44,502 --> 00:00:47,393 [NOISE] thank you, thank you very much.	00:00:01,111 --> 00:00:16,258 [خطأ: لدينا 2000] لدينا استراتيجية رعاية [كرنش] في مرحلة الاحتضار في العام 2008 ونحن نريد أن نحرص على أن نتطرق إلى كل المجالات. 00:00:16,258 --> 00:00:30,510 [تنفس] لقد تحدث الدكتور [علم: شخص غالي] عن كلفة مرحلة الاحتضار و[تنفس] هناك الموت في البيت أو الميت في قطاع معين في وضعية معينة. 00:00:30,510 --> 00:00:40,413 [تنفس] في أغلب الأحيان نحن نتخذ الخيارات الخاطئة ربما اتخذ القرارات أو الخيارات الجيدة [تنفس] [إعادة: لا] لا تعتمد على المال. 00:00:40,413 --> 00:00:52,331 بل [تنفس] الخيارات هي التي تعود إلى رغبة المريض فعلاً والذي عبر عنها شكراً. [إعادة: شكرًا] شكرًا جزيلاً أنتقل الآن إلى المتحدثة الثانية.

Figure 2: Original Speaker's vs Interpreter's Transcripts Segmentation Differences.

The segmentation difference was one of the difficulties we encountered on our way to manually annotating the transcripts. Our solution is explained in Section 5.

The different number of *Words* between English and Arabic, which can be observed in Table 1 is another very interesting point. As Arabic is an agglutinative language, it has fewer words. Thus, it has been observed that the average ratio between English and Arabic words in the original texts and their translations is around 1.5 (Salameh et al., 2011). We have computed this ratio both for the transcripts (original vs interpreted, as visible in Figure 1 horizontally, i.e. A1 vs B1), and for the manual translations vs the transcripts (vertically, A1 vs B2 and B1 vs A2) to test if this ratio is confirmed in our cases. We have found that vertically, in A1 vs B2 and B1 vs A2, the average ratios are around 1.5, which confirms the previously observed, and that there is a very small divergence. However, Table 1 shows that horizontally, the ratio

Language	N. of files	Total Time	N. of Segments	N. of Words	N. of Words Translation
Arabic	133	31:54:33	9,555	159,657	198,588
English	133	31:54:33	26,824	289,109	224,296
Totals.	266	63:49:05	36,379	448,766	422,884

Table 1: WAW Corpus' Size.

between English and Arabic words in interpreters' vs original speakers' transcripts is higher, around **1.8** (289,109/159,657 = 1.81). Our hypothesis is that interpreters add more words than translators do.

Figure 3 shows the horizontal (A1 vs B1) word ratios for each interpreter. Comparing to the results for manual translations, where there is less variety and all ratios tend to be close to 1.5, we see larger differences for some interpreters (longer colored rectangle). This shows that the same interpreter added a different number of words in Arabic vs. English in the different speeches he/she interpreted. E.g. interpreters I07 and I09 have the largest variety, while I01 and I08 have the smallest variety.

This word ratios higher variety further motivated our wish to have a more detailed look into the behaviour of single interpreters via manual annotation (see Sections 6 and 7).

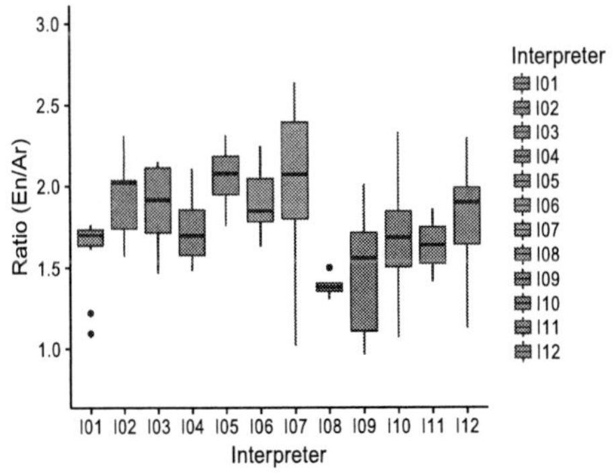

Figure 3: Word Ratios between Original Speakers' transcripts and Interpreters' Transcripts, per Interpreter.

5 Document Segmentation and Alignment

As said earlier, **the original segmentation difference was *one of the difficulties* on our way**, as we wanted to align parallel segments so the annotator annotates both the original and the interpretation segments in parallel, and later we learn automatically the segments correspondence.

Table 2 shows examples of files from the same session/lectures. E.g., File 2 has 286 English segments, and only 94 Arabic segments. The same happens with all the files.

For our annotation experiment, we worked on a corpus sample, composed by the parts of 4 files with a total of 7500 words, interpreted by 2 interpreters (I09 and I10). I10 did the most interpretations across the three conferences. This made us hypothesize that he/she was the most expert. I09 had the average words ratio closest to written translation (1.5) and had a high words ratio variety. We hypothesized that this interpreter could be a beginner.

First, we attempted to automatically re-align the texts using automatic alignment tools (Varga et al., 2006; Ma, 2010; Braune and Fraser, 2010). The results were unsatisfactory as interpreters change both the word order and lexical choice by paraphrasing or summarizing the original speaker, so alignment tools could not find enough parallel segments.

Manual re-segmentation and alignment was done by one expert, native speaker of Arabic with advanced level of English, who was a specialist in video subtitles segmentation. The process took in total 7h 49min 16sec. Besides the obvious learning curve for this highly specific task, the average speed was 0.17 English w/sec (words/second) and 0.10 Arabic w/sec.

***Another difficulty* was finding an appropriate tool for both re-segmentation, alignment, and annotation**. We split this task into 1. Re-segmentation and alignment and 2. Annotation. For (1), our expert used Excel spreadsheet and then our in-house web-based editing tool which better visualizes the parallel segments and outputs an unique merged file. The procedure was to 1. Segment the original speaker's transcript, 2. Align and segment the interpreter's transcript, according to (1).

File	Interpreter	time (sec)	En Segments	En Words	Ar Segments	Ar Words	Ratio
1	I10	231	43	559	19	331	1.69
2	I09	1296	286	3315	94	1963	1.69
3	I10	2050	444	5557	163	2386	2.33
4	I09	1101	274	3147	89	1728	1.82

Table 2: Expert Evaluation Data.

Initially, we followed video subtitles segmentation rules, but this resulted in too short segments, which created problems for aligning, as often the interpreters were changing the whole structure and the order of clauses and phrases.

Next, we have set as main rule to have an aligned segment in Arabic, while keeping the length of the original English sentence as short as possible.

The manually re-segmented and aligned version of Figure 2 is shown in Figure 4. The empty lines are left when there is no correspondence in the other language.

The final WAW re-segmentation and alignment guidelines are available online[4].

great importance we had a 2008 end-of-life care strategy	لدينا 2000 لدينا استراتيجية رعاية في مرحلة الاحتضار في العام 2008
which we now are in the process of refreshing	
and we are needing to ensure that we attack each of those three areas.	ونحن نريد أن نحرص على أن نتطرق إلى كل المجالات.
Dr. Ghali referred to other issues about the cost of end-of-life care	لقد تحدث الدكتور غالي عن كلفة مرحلة الاحتضار
and that is also really critical in the choice as to the home death	و هناك الموت في البيت
or the death in an acute setting with expensive intervention occurring.	أو الميت في قطاع معين في وضعية معينة.
too often we make the inappropriate choice.	في أغلب الأحيان نحن نتخذ الخيارات الخاطئة
to make the right choice is not one to be dictated by money;	ربما اتخاذ القرارات أ و الخيارات الجيدة لا لا تعتمد على المال.
it is to make a choice that reflects the real wishes as quotably expressed by the patient.	بل الخيارات هي التي تعود إلى رغبة المريض فعلاً والذي عبر عنها
thank you.	شكراً.
thank you, thank you very much.	شكرًا شكرًا جزيلاً

Figure 4: Manually Re-Segmented and Re-Aligned Transcript.

6 Annotation

Our **annotator** was a professional translator with expertise in annotating translation strategies, native speaker of Arabic, and fluent in English. The annotator passed a training on annotating around 1500 words. Training annotation was done using Word. Four strategies have been explored: *Summarizing*, *Omission affecting the meaning*, *Omission not affecting the meaning* and *Correction.*

The **annotation categories** for main annotation were selected: 1) out of the interpreting strategies listed in the Section 2, 2) filtered during annotator's training, 3) coarse-grained. We have also asked the expert to evaluate whether some of these strategies were **needed** ("*tolerant*") or **unnecessary** ("*intolerant*"). Our final annotation categories are: *Summarizing*, *Omissions (tolerant, out-of-delay*, and *intolerant*), *intolerant Additions*, and *Self-correction.*

Finding an annotation tool was also one of our difficulties, as we needed to find a way for both aligned segments to be annotated in parallel. After asking in corpora mailing list [5], we found our own solution. After producing a merged file (Section 5) with both parallel segments one after the other, we used GATE [6]. Our annotation guidelines are available online [7] .

Four files with a total of 4941 words in English and respectively 2767 words in Arabic were annotated. The source language in all files was English and the target – Arabic. Here are our annotation categories with their (expert's) definitions and an example for each category.

Summarizing (Table 3): The interpreter combines two clauses into one clause capturing the main idea and conforming to the structure of Arabic. A single longer clause may also be summarized by the interpreter.

Original Speaker's Transcript	Interpreter's Transcript
So for instance we now from my group have spin out, they do mental health assessment	في مجموعتي مثلاً قمنا بتقييم الصحة النفسية *Translation: In my group, for instance, we assessed the psychological health.*

Table 3: Summarizing Strategy Example

Self-correction (Table 4): The interpreter usually uses "أو" (or) or repetition to alter a lexical choice or correct a mispronounced word.

[4]Link: `http://goo.gl/hjyhAz.`

[5]https://mailman.uib.no/public/corpora/2017-May/026526.html.

[6]https://gate.ac.uk/.

[7]Link: `http://goo.gl/hjyhAz.`

Original Speaker's Transcript	Interpreter's Transcript
We know where to focus on our clinical interventions.	علينا أن نكون مركزين أكثر في مُداخل أو في تدخلاتنا السريرية. *Translation:We have to be more concentrated on interventions or on our clinical interventions.*

Table 4: Self-correction Strategy Example

Omission-tolerant (Table 5): This strategy is used when the information introduced by the speaker seems to not have essential effect on the entire meaning of the context. May also result from the speakers frequent repetitions of the same idea or clause.

Original Speaker's Transcript	Interpreter's Transcript
Thank you very much.	

Table 5: Omission-tolerant Strategy Example

Omission-intolerant (Table 6): These omissions affect the overall meaning of the context. They stem from interpreter's delay, miscomprehension, lack of anticipation, or/and the speaker's speed.

Original Speaker's Transcript	Interpreter's Transcript
So I deal with individuals who have traditional, you can say traditional cultural values	وأنا أتعاطى بالمسائل الثقافية الإسلامية *Translation: And I deal with Islamic cultural questions/ issues.*

Table 6: Omission-intolerant Strategy Example

Omission-out of delay-intolerant (Table 7): This omission usually results from a long period of delay. The interpreter loses information because he/she may be unable to comprehend what is being said or because of the speaker's speed.

Addition-unnecessary (Table 8): The interpreter adds information that seems out of context (usually happens out of delay). However, some interpreters use this strategy to provide more explanations to the audience.

7 Annotation Results

182 instances out of 1047 segments were annotated (around 17%). Out of these, 135 were "*Omission*"; 21 were "*Addition*"; 16 "*Self-correction*" and 10 "*Summarizing*". Figure 5 shows the tags distribution per file. The annotation provided some insights about our initial observations. In the cases when the num. of words ratio was high (File 3 in Table 2), the annotations showed a high amount of "*Omissions*" in the Arabic interpretation vs. the original English speech. "*Summarizing*" contributes to this too, as shown in Figure 5. *Omissions* are the major cause of information loss "*Addition*" and "*Self-correction*" could balance this loss, but they are a too low number to compensate. File 1 was an exception. The length of the file (231 sec only, vs. 1000-2000 sec the other files, each) could potentially be the reason why we did not observe much.

Original Speaker's Transcript	Interpreter's Transcript
And they examined it, and they came out	
They were extremely concerned about the Dutch system	
And also the system in Oregon and some of the states in the United States.	

Table 7: Omission-out-of-delay-intolerant Strategy Example

Original Speaker's Transcript	Interpreter's Transcript
I did some work for our Royal College of Physicians on professionalism	أنا أتحدث دائمًا عن المهنية والاحتراف *Translation: I am always taking about being professional and professionalism*
And we thought very deep and hard about what is professionalism.	ونحن نفكر بعمق عما هي المهنية، *Translation: And we think deeply about what is professionalism*

Table 8: Addition unnecessary Strategy Example

8 Conclusions & Future Work

The WAW corpus is a collection of parallel lectures translated and interpreted from English into Arabic (mostly) and vice-versa. In the process of exploiting this resource for teaching a S2T automatic translation system, we investigated the characteristics of professional interpretation. An expert translator annotated the professional interpreters' strategies in a sample of the corpus by following our guidelines to segment, align and an-

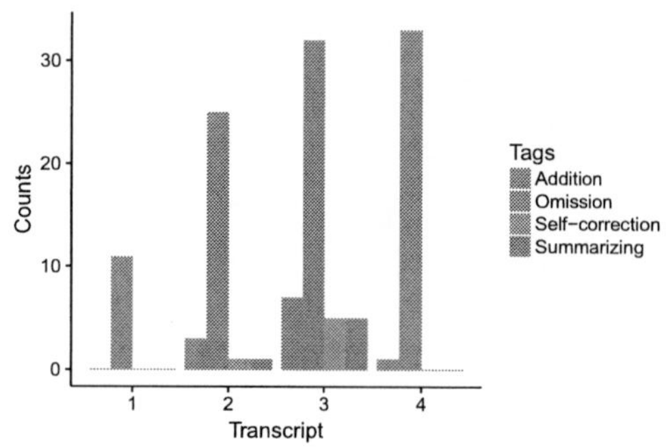

Figure 5: Distribution of Annotation Tags per Transcript.

notate the transcripts. The findings from this pilot experiment confirmed and explained the previously observed anomalies. The discovered strategies will be tested within our in-house S2T translation system. The WAW corpus can be used by student interpreters to learn real, quality interpretation, by researchers in related fields, as well as to improve MT. We aim to expand these tasks further, as well as to automatize some of the previous steps. For future work, we are in the process of involving more annotators, better defining the annotation guidelines, and processing more texts.

References

Raja Al-Khanji, Said El-Shiyab, and Riyadh Hussein. 2000. On the use of compensatory strategies in simultaneous interpretation. *Meta: Journal des traducteurs/Meta: Translators' Journal* 45(3):548–557.

Magdalena Bartłomiejczyk. 2006. Strategies of simultaneous interpreting and directionality. *Interpreting* 8(2):149–174.

Claudio Bendazzoli and Annalisa Sandrelli. 2009. Corpus-based interpreting studies: Early work and future prospects. *Tradumàtica: traducció i tecnologies de la informació i la comunicació* (7).

Fabienne Braune and Alexander Fraser. 2010. Improved unsupervised sentence alignment for symmetrical and asymmetrical parallel corpora. In *Proceedings of the 23rd International Conference on Computational Linguistics: Posters*. Association for Computational Linguistics, pages 81–89.

Fahim Dalvi, Yifan Zhang, Sameer Khurana, Nadir Durrani, Hassan Sajjad, Ahmed Abdelali, Hamdy Mubarak, Ahmed Ali, and Stephan Vogel. 2017. Qcri live speech translation system. *EACL 2017* page 61.

Christa Hauenschild and Susanne Heizmann. 1997. *Machine translation and translation theory*, volume 1. Walter de Gruyter.

He He, Jordan L Boyd-Graber, and Hal Daumé III. 2016. Interpretese vs. translationese: The uniqueness of human strategies in simultaneous interpretation. In *HLT-NAACL*. pages 971–976.

Kaibao Hu. 2016. Corpus-based interpreting studies. In *Introducing Corpus-based Translation Studies*, Springer, pages 193–221.

William John Hutchins and Harold L Somers. 1992. *An introduction to machine translation*, volume 362. Academic Press, London.

Sylvia Kalina. 1998. *Strategische Prozesse beim Dolmetschen: Theoretische Grundlagen, empirische Fallstudien, didaktische Konsequenzen*, volume 18. G. Narr.

Judith F Kroll and Annette MB De Groot. 2009. *Handbook of bilingualism: Psycholinguistic approaches*. Oxford University Press.

Marianne Lederer. 1978. Simultaneous interpretationunits of meaning and other features. In *Language interpretation and communication*, Springer, pages 323–332.

Konstantina Liontou. 1996. Strategies in German-to-Greek simultaneous interpreting: A corpus-based approach. *Gramma: Journal of Theory & Criticism* 19:37–56.

Konstantina Liontou. 2012. *Anticipation in German to Greek simultaneous interpreting*. Ph.D. thesis, Uniwien.

Xiaoyi Ma. 2010. Champollion: A robust parallel text sentence aligner. In *LREC 2006: Fifth International Conference on Language Resources and Evaluation*. pages 489–492.

Matthias Paulik and Alex Waibel. 2009. Automatic translation from parallel speech: Simultaneous interpretation as mt training data. In *Automatic Speech Recognition & Understanding, 2009. ASRU 2009. IEEE Workshop on*. IEEE, pages 496–501.

Jones Roderick. 2002. *Conference Interpreting Explained (Translation Practices Explained)*. St. Jerome Publishing.

Mohammad Salameh, Rached Zantout, and Nashat Mansour. 2011. Improving the accuracy of english-arabic statistical sentence alignment. In *Int. Arab J. Inf. Technol.*. volume 8, pages 171–177.

Hiroaki Shimizu, Graham Neubig, Sakriani Sakti, Tomoki Toda, and Satoshi Nakamura. 2013. Constructing a speech translation system using simultaneous interpretation data. In *Proceedings of International Workshop on Spoken Language Translation (IWSLT)*.

Miriam Shlesinger. 1998. Corpus-based interpreting studies as an offshoot of corpus-based translation studies. *Meta: journal des traducteurs/Meta: Translators' Journal* 43(4):486–493.

Vivek Kumar Rangarajan Sridhar, John Chen, and Srinivas Bangalore. 2013. Corpus analysis of simultaneous interpretation data for improving real time speech translation. In *INTERSPEECH*. pages 3468–3472.

Hitomi Tohyama and Shigeki Matsubara. 2006. Collection of simultaneous interpreting patterns by using bilingual spoken monologue corpus. In *Proceedings of the Language Resources and Evaluation Conference (LREC)*.

Dániel Varga, László Németh, P. Halcsy, András Kornai, Viktor Trón, and Viktor Nagy. 2006. Parallel corpora for medium density languages. In *Proceedings of the RANLP 2005*. pages 590–596.

Binhua Wang. 2012. Interpreting strategies in real-life interpreting .

Translation Memory Systems Have a Long Way to Go

Andrea Silvestre Baquero[1], Ruslan Mitkov[2]
[1]Polytechnic University of Valencia, [2]University of Wolverhampton
andreasilvestre4@gmail.com, r.mitkov@wlv.ac.uk

Abstract

The TM memory systems changed the work of translators and now the translators not benefiting from these tools are a tiny minority. These tools operate on fuzzy (surface) matching mostly and cannot benefit from already translated texts which are synonymous to (or paraphrased versions of) the text to be translated. The match score is mostly based on character-string similarity, calculated through Levenshtein distance. The TM tools have difficulties with detecting similarities even in sentences which represent a minor revision of sentences already available in the translation memory. This shortcoming of the current TM systems was the subject of the present study and was empirically proven in the experiments we conducted. To this end, we compiled a small translation memory (English-Spanish) and applied several lexical and syntactic transformation rules to the source sentences with both English and Spanish being the source language.

The results of this study show that current TM systems have a long way to go and highlight the need for TM systems equipped with NLP capabilities which will offer the translator the advantage of he/she not having to translate a sentence again if an almost identical sentence has already been already translated.

1. Introduction

While automatic translation has taken off to work reasonably in some scenarios and to do well for gisting purposes, even today, against the background of the latest promising results delivered by statistical Machine Translation (MT) systems such as Google Translate and latest developments in Neural Machine Translation and in general Deep Learning for MT, automatic translation gets it often wrong and is not good enough for professional translation. Consequently, there has been a pressing need for a new generation of tools for professional translators to assist them reliably and speed up the translation process. Historically, it was Krollman who first put forward the reuse of existing human translations in 1971. A few years later, in 1979 Arthern went further and proposed the retrieval and reuse not only of identical text fragments (exact matches) but also of similar source sentences and their translations (fuzzy matches). It took another decade before the ideas sketched by Krollman and Arthern were commercialised as a result of the development of various computer-aided translation (CAT) tools such as Translation Memory (TM) systems in the early 1990s. These translation tools revolutionised the work of translators and the last two decades saw dramatic changes in the translation workflow.

The TM memory systems indeed changed the work of translators and now the translators not benefiting from these tools are a tiny minority. However, while these tools have proven to be very efficient for repetitive and voluminous texts, they operate on fuzzy (surface) matching mostly and cannot benefit from already translated texts which are synonymous to (or paraphrased versions of) the text to be translated. The match score is mostly based on character-string similarity, calculated through Levenshtein distance ("measure of the minimum number of insertions, deletions and substitutions needed to change one sequence of letters into another."; Somers 2003)

The limitations of the traditional TM systems in terms of matching have been highlighted by a number of authors. By way of example, Somers (2003) gives the example below to illustrate one drawback:

a. Select 'Symbol' in the Insert menu.
b. Select 'Symbol' in the Insert menu to enter character from the symbol set.
c. Select 'Paste' in the Edit menu.

The Proceedings of the First Workshop on Human-Informed Translation and Interpreting Technology (HiT-IT), pages 44–51,
Varna, Bulgaria, Sept 7, 2017

Given the input sentence (a), (c) would be the highest match percentage, as it differs in only two words, while (b) has eight additional words. Intuitively (b) is a better match since it includes the text of (a) in its entirety.

Before Mitkov (2005) elaborated on the specific matching limitations of TM systems, Macklovitch and Russel (2000) pointed out 'Current Translation Memory technology is limited by the rudimentary techniques employed for approximate matching'. They went on to illustrate that unless an TM system can do morphological analysis, it will have difficult recognising that (f) is more similar to (d) than (e):

d. The wild child is destroying his new toy
e. The wild chief is destroying his new tool
f. The wild children are destroying their new toy

Gow (2003) notes that SDL Trados gives the segments 'Prendre des mesures de dotation et de classification.' and 'Connaissance des techniques de rédaction et de révision.' a match rating of as high as 56% even though the above sentences have nothing to do with each other the reason being that because half of the words are the same and they are in the same position, even though the common words are only function words.

Recent work on new generation TM systems (Gupta 2015; Gupta et al. 2016a; Gupta et al. 2016b; Timonera and Mitkov 2015; Gupta and Orasan 2014) show that when NLP techniques such as paraphrasing or clause splitting are applied, TM systems performance is enhanced.

While that it is clear that TM systems are incapable of any linguistic or semantic interpretation, we maintain that they have difficulties with detecting similarities even in sentences which represent a minor revision of sentences already available in the translation memory. In order to substantiate this claim empirically, we conducted the following experiments.

We conducted experiments using a small translation memory (English-Spanish) in which we apply several lexical and syntactic transformation rules to the source sentences – both for English and Spanish serving as source language. The transformation rules are selected in such a way that they are simple and the transformed sentences do not change in meaning. The hypothesis of this study is that in many cases the TM systems cannot detect the fact that the transformed sentences are practically the same as sentences already translated as the match computed is below the threshold. This in turn, would mean insufficient efficiency as the new, practically the same sentences, will have to be translated again. For the purpose of this study we experimented with the well-known TM systems Trados, Wordfast, Omega T and MemoQ.

2. Data Description

For the purpose of this experiment a translation memory or alternatively parallel corpora were needed. To this end, we compiled a parallel English-Spanish corpus consisting of online documents of the European Union and the United Nations. The English documents selected were *Charter of the Fundamental Rights*, *Declaration on the Right to Development*, *Declaration on the Rights of Persons Belonging to National or Ethnic, and Religious and Linguistic Minorities*, *United Nations Declaration on the Rights of Indigenous People*, and *Universal Declaration of Human Rights*. We also selected the Spanish equivalents of these documents: *Carta de los derechos fundamentals de la Unión Europea*, *Declaración de las Naciones Unidades sobre el derecho al desarrollo*, *Declaración sobres los derechos de las personas pertenecientes a minorías nacionales o étnicas, religiosas y lingüísticas*, *Declaración de las Naciones Unidades sobre los derechos de los pueblos indígena* and *Declaración universal de los derechos humanos*.[1] The size of the English corpus was 14,153 words while the size of the Spanish corpus is 15,461 words (for more details see Table 1).

[1] The documents in English and Spanish are identical in contents even though the titles are slightly different.

English documents		Spanish documents	
Name	Size	Name	Size
1. Charter of the Fundamental Rights of the European Union	4,143	1. Carta de los derechos fundamentales de la Unión Europea	4,357
2. United Nations on the Right to Development	1,926	2. Declaración de las Naciones Unidas sobre el derecho al desarrollo	2,166
3. United Nation Declaration on the Rights of Indigenous Peoples	4,001	3. Declaración de las Naciones Unidas sobre los pueblos indígenas	4,427
4. Declaration on the Rights of Persons Belonging to National or Ethnic, Religious and Linguistic Minorities	2,309	4. Declaración sobre los derechos de las personas pertenecientes a minorías nacionales o étnicas, religiosas y lingüísticas	2,552
5. Universal Declaration of Human Rights	1,778	5. Declaración Universal de Derechos Humanos	1,959
Total documents : 5	Total words: 14,153	Total documents : 5	Total words: 15,461

Table 1: The experimental translation memory

We are aware the compiled corpus is very small but we regard this study and results as preliminary. In fact for the purpose of our experiments we selected a small sample of 150 aligned sentences in English and Spanish; this 'experimental TM' served as a basis for the experiments outlined.

3. Transformations

For the purpose of this study, we developed 10 transformation rules. Rule 1 was to transform an original sentence in active voice into a passive voice sentence, if possible. Rule 2 was a mirror image of rule 1 – transform a sentence in passive voice into active voice sentence. Rule 3 had to do with changing the order inside the sentence – changing the order of words, phrases or clauses within a sentence. Rule 4 sought to replace a word with a synonym whereas Rule 5 replaced 2 words of a sentence with their synonyms. The replacement with synonyms was applied to nouns, verbs and adverbs and in cases where the existence of synonym with identical meaning was 'obvious'. Rule 6 built on rule 3 by changing the order within a sentence but in addition replaced a noun with a pronoun for which it served as antecedent. Rule 7 was a combination of rule 1 and 4 – change of active voice into passive and replacement of a word with its synonym. Rule 8 changed passive voice into passive and like rule 6 - noun with a coreferential pronoun. Rule 9 was combination of rule 3 and rule 5, and finally was a subsequent application of rule 2, rule 3 and pronominalisation of a noun.

Table 2 below lists the rules with examples in English, whereas Table 3 lists the rules with examples in Spanish.

Rule	Transformation	Original sentence (English)	Transformed sentence (English)
1	Change active to passive voice	States must take measures to protect and promote the rights of minorities and their identity.	Measures must be taken to protect and promote the rights of minorities and their identity.
2	Change passive to active voice	The history, traditions and cultures of minorities must be reflected in education.	The education must reflect the history, traditions and cultures of minorities.
3	Change word order, phrase order or clause order	Reaffirming those indigenous peoples, in the exercise of their rights, should be free from discrimination of any kind.	Reaffirming those indigenous peoples should be free from discrimination of any kind, in the exercise of their rights.
4	Replace one word with its synonym	Everyone has the right to	Every person has the right to

		nationality.	nationality.
5	Replace two words with its synonym	Respect for the rights of the defence of anyone who has been changed shall be guaranteed.	Consideration for the rights of the protection of anyone who has been changed shall be guaranteed.
6	Replace one word into a pronoun AND change word order, phrase order or clause order	Indigenous peoples have the right to access, without any discrimination, to all social and health services.	They also have the right to access to all social and health services without any discrimination.
7	Change active to passive voice AND replace one word with its synonym	All children, whether born in or out of wedlock, shall enjoy the same social protection.	The identical social protection shall be enjoyed by all children, whether born in or out wedlock.
8	Change passive to active voice AND replace one word into a pronoun	No one shall be arbitrarily deprived of his property.	It shall not arbitrary deprive.
9	Change word order, phrase order or clause order AND replace two words with their synonyms	This booklet captures the essence of the Declaration, which is printed in full in this publication.	This brochure is printed in full in this publication which captures the nature of the Declaration.
10	Change active to passive voice AND change word order, phrase order or clause order AND replace one word into a pronoun	Enjoyment of these rights entails responsibilities and duties with regard to other persons, to human community and to future generations.	By enjoyment of these rights is involved the responsibilities and duties with regard to them, to the human community and to forthcoming generations.

Table 2: Transformation rules and examples in English

Rule	Transformation	Original sentence (Spanish)	Transformed sentence (Spanish)
1	Change active to passive voice	Destacando que corresponde a las Naciones Unidas desempeñar un papel importante y continuo de promoción y protección de los derechos de los pueblos indígenas.	Destacando que es correspondido por las Naciones Unidades desempeñar un papel importante y continuo de promoción y protección de los derechos de los pueblos indígenas.
2	Change passive to active voice	El contacto pacífico entre minorías no debe ser restringido.	Los Estados no deben restringir el contacto pacífico entre minorías.
3	Change word order, phrase order or clause order	Los Estados, sin perjuicio de la obligación de expresión, deberán alentar a los medios de información privados a reflejar debidamente la diversidad cultural indígena.	Los Estados deberán alentar a los medios de información privados a reflejar debidamente la diversidad indígena, sin perjuicio de la obligación de asegurar plenamente la libertad de expresión.
4	Replace one word with its synonym	Se garantiza la protección de la familia en los planos jurídico, económico y social.	Se asegura la protección de la familia en los planos jurídico, económico y social.
5	Replace two words with its synonym	Las sociedades de todo el mundo disfrutan de la diversidad étnica, lingüística y religiosa.	Las sociedades mundiales disfrutan de la variedad étnica, lingüística y religiosa.
6	Replace one word into a pronoun AND change word order, phrase order or clause order	Todos los niños, nacidos de matrimonio o fuera de matrimonio, tienen derecho a igual protección social.	Ellos tienen derechos a igual protección social, nacidos de matrimonio o fuera de matrimonio.
7	Change active to passive voice AND replace one word with its synonym	Los Estados tomarán las medidas que sean necesarias para lograr progresivamente que este derecho se haga plenamente efectivo.	Las decisiones que sean necesarias para lograr progresivamente que este derecho se haga plenamente efectivo serán tomadas por los Estados.

8	Change passive to active voice AND replace one word into a pronoun	La igualdad entre hombres y mujeres será garantizada en todos los ámbitos, inclusive en materia de empleo, trabajo y retribución.	Ellos garantizarán la igualdad entre hombres y mujeres en todos los ámbitos, inclusive en materia de empleo, trabajo y retribución.
9	Change word order, phrase order or clause order AND replace two words with their synonyms	Del ejercicio de ese derecho no puede resultar discriminación de ningún tipo.	No puede surgir discriminación de ningún tipo de la actuación del ejercicio de ese derecho.
10	Change active to passive voice AND change word order, phrase order or clause order AND replace one word into a pronoun	Al definirse y ejecutarse todas las políticas y acciones de la Unión se garantizará un alto nivel de protección de la salud humana.	Un alto nivel de protección de la salud humana será garantizada al ejecutarse y definirse todas las políticas y acciones de ella.

Table 3: Transformation rules and examples in Spanish

4. Experiments, Results and Discussion

We use the above parallel corpus as a translation memory and experiment with both English and Spanish as source languages. If we had to translate again a sentence from the source Language, the match would be obviously 100%. For the purpose of the experiment, each sentence of the source text undergoes a transformation after applying the rules listed below, which convert the original sentences into syntactically different but semantically same sentences. As the new sentences have the same meaning, it would be desirable that the TM systems produce a high match between the transformed sentences and the original ones. By 'high match' we mean a match above the threshold of a specific TM tool so that the user can benefit from the translation of the original sentence being displayed.

Rule	# Sentences	Trados		Wordfast		OmegaT		MemoQ	
		< 75%	Failure %	<75%	Failure%	<75%	Failure%	<75%	Failure%
1	28	10	35.71	2	7.14	14	50	11	39.28
2	27	7	25.92	6	22.2	14	51.85	13	48.15
3	84	8	9.52	0	0	18	21.43	24	28.57
4	150	2	1.33	21	14	6	4	13	8.6
5	150	10	6.67	77	51	7	4.6	62	41.3
6	29	11	37.93	5	17.24	14	48.27	16	55.17
7	26	9	34.61	14	53.85	11	42.31	22	84.61
8	9	2	22.22	3	33.3	5	55.55	6	66.67
9	84	22	26.19	42	50	42	50	64	76.2
10	20	4	20	5	25	9	45	14	70

Table 4: Matching results English

The results obtained with English as a source language show that the lexical and syntactic transformations cause significant problems to the TM systems and their inability to return matching above the default threshold means that the translator may miss out on the re-use of translations he/she has already made. In the case of Trados there are as many as 36% of the sentences not being returned after being transformed with rule 1; this figure goes up to 38% when applying rule 6 and 35% with rule 7. Wordfast fails to propose similarity for 54% of the sentences once rule 7 is applied. As for Omega T, the application of rule 8 results in

56% of the transformed sentences not being detected as similar to the original sentence. MemoQ's failures are even more dramatic in that the applications of rules 10, 9 and 7 leads to inability to detected similarity in 70%, 76% and 85% of the cases respectively! Overall, MemoQ reports the most negative results which is surprising given the very positive feedback of users in general for this tool.

It appears that TM systems in general have more problems with syntactic transformations – after applying rules 1, 2, 3 or the combined rules 6-10. The TM systems also report fewer problems for lexical transformation only – e.g. after applying rules 4 and 5 only.

As the transformations are language specific, we conducted similar experiments with Spanish being the source languages. We transformed the original Spanish sentences using the above rules and the TM systems computed the match between the transformed sentences and the original ones.

Rule	# Sentences	Trados		Wordfast		OmegaT		MemoQ	
		<75%	Failure %	<75%	Failure%	<75%	Failure%	#<75%	Failure%
1	50	10	20	7	14	22	44	12	24
2	18	11	61.1	10	55.55	11	61.11	12	66.67
3	91	20	21.98	1	1.10	19	20.88	23	25.27
4	150	5	3.33	24	16	5	5	14	9.33
5	150	13	8.67	95	63.3	33	22	55	36.67
6	44	18	40.9	5	11.36	16	36.36	20	45.45
7	50	16	32	29	58	19	38	24	48
8	17	10	58.82	8	47.05	10	58.82	9	52.94
9	91	36	39.56	50	54.94	41	45.05	55	60.44
10	25	6	24	9	36	9	36	18	72

Table 5: Matching results Spanish

The results obtained with Spanish as a source language show that the lexical and syntactic transformations cause more significant problems to the TM systems than with English as a source language. In the case of Trados there are as many as 40% of the sentences not being returned after being transformed with rule 6 and 9; this figure goes up around 60% when applying rule 8 and 61% with rule 2. Wordfast fails to propose similarity for around 55% of the sentences once rule 2 and 9 are applied; and up to 63% when rule 5 is also applied. As for Omega T, the application of rule 8 results in 59% of the transformed sentences not being detected as similar to the original sentence and up to 61% when applying rule 2. MemoQ's failures after applying rules 8, 9 and 2 leads to inability of detecting similarity in 52%, 60% and 67% of the different cases. On the whole, every TM system exhibits retrieval failures mostly related to combining different rules.

It is worth noting the high errors rates for all TM systems even with rule 2 which confirms their inability to deal with syntactic transformations.

Finally, it is worth observing that for Spanish as source language the matching failures are higher. As the above TM systems have no NLP functionalities and usually use Levenstein distance as a matching algorithm, we conjecture that this has to do with the slightly more complex syntax in Spanish.

5. Conclusion

Current TM systems have a long way to go. The above results highlight the need for TM technology to embrace NLP techniques such as parsing or paraphrasing. A TM system equipped with NLP capabilities will offer the translator the advantage of he/she not having to translate a sentence again if an almost identical sentence has already been already translated.

References

Arthern, Peter. 1979. "Machine translation and computerised terminology systems: a translator's viewpoint." Edited by Barbara Snell. Translating and the computer Amsterdam, North-Holland. 77-108.

Gow, Francie. 2003. "Metrics for Evaluating Translation Memory Software." MA thesis, University of Ottawa, Canada.

Grönroos, Mickel, and Ari Becks. 2005. "Bringing Intelligence to Translation Memory Technology." Proceedings of the International Conference Translating and the Computer 27. London: ASLIB.

Gupta, R. 2015. *Use of Language technology to improve matching and retrieval in Translation Memory*. PhD thesis. University of Wolverampton.

Gupta, R., Orasan, C., Zampieri, M., Vela. M., Mihaela Vela, van Genabith, J. and R. Mitkov. 2016a. "Improving Translation Memory matching and retrieval using paraphrases", *Machine Translation*, 30(1), 19-40.

Gupta, R., Orasan, C., Liu, Q. and R. Mitkov. 2016b. A Dynamic Programming Approach to Improving Translation Memory Matching and Retrieval using Paraphrases. In *Proceedings of the 19th International Conference on Text, Speech and Dialogue (TSD)*, Brno, Czech Republic.

Gupta, R. and Orasan, C. 2014. Incorporating Paraphrasing in Translation Memory Matching and Retrieval. In *Proceedings of the Seventeenth Annual Conference of the European Association for Machine Translation (EAMT2014)*, 3-10. Dubrovnik, Croatia.

Gupta, R., Bechara, H. and C. Orasan. 2014. "Intelligent Translation Memory Matching and Retrieval Metric Exploiting Linguistic Technology". *Proceedings of the Translating and Computer 36*, 86-89.

Hodász, Gábor, and Gábor Pohl. 2005. "MetaMorpho TM: a linguistically enriched translation memory." Edited by Walter Hahn, John Hutchins and Cristina Vertan. International Workshop, Modern Approaches in Translation Technologies..

Hutchins, John. 1998. "The origins of the translator's workstation." Machine Translation 13, n° 4: 287-307.

Kay, Martin. 1980. "The Proper Place of Men and Machines in Language Translation." Machine Translation 12, n° 1-2: 3-23.

Lagoudaki, Pelagia Maria. 2008. "Expanding the Possibilities of Translation Memory Systems: From the Translator's Wishlist to the Developer's Design." PhD diss., Imperial College of London

Lagoudaki, Pelagia Maria. 2006. "Translation Memories Survey 2006: Users' perceptions around TM use." Translating and the Computer 28 (ASLIB).

Macklovitch, Elliott, and Graham Russell. 2000. "What's Been Forgotten in Translation Memory." AMTA '00 Proceedings of the 4th Conference of the Association for Machine Translation in the Americas on Envisioning Machine Translation in the Information Future. London: Springer-Verlag.137-146.

Marsye, Aurora. 2011. "Towards a New Generation Translation Memory: A Paraphrase Recognition Study for Translation Memory System Development." Master's Thesis. University of Wolverhampton and Université de Franche-Comté..

Mitkov, Ruslan, and Gloria Corpas. 2008. "Improving Third Generation Translation Memory systems through identification of rhetorical predicates." Proceedings of the LangTech 2008 conference. Rome,

Mitkov, Ruslan. 2005. 'New Generation Translation Memory systems'. Panel discussion at the 27th international Aslib conference 'Translating and the Computer'. London

Pekar, Viktor, and Ruslan Mitkov. 2007. "New Generation Translation Memory: Content-Sensitive Matching." Proceedings of the 40th Anniversary Congress of the Swiss Association of Translators, Terminologists and Interpreters. Bern: ASTTI

Nicolas, Lionel, Egon Stemle, Klara Kranebitter and Verena Lyding. 2013. " High-Accuracy Phrase Translation Acquisition through Battle-Royale Selection ". Proceedings of RANLP'2013.

Planas, Emmanuel, and Osamu Furuse. 1999. "Formalizing Translation Memories." Proc MT Summit VII. 331-339.

Planas, Emmanuel. 2005. "SIMILIS: Second-generation translation memory software." proceedings of the 27th International Conference Translating and the Computer. London: Reinke, Uwe. State of the Art in Translation Memory Technology. 2013. *Translation: Computation, Corpora, Cognition*, [S.l.], v. 3, n. 1, jun. 2013. ISSN 2193-6986.

Somers, Harold. "Translation Memory Systems." 2003. In Computers and Translation: A Translator's Guide, Edited by Harold Somers,

31-47. Amsterdam/Philadelphia: John Benjamins Publishing Company.

Steinberger, Ralf, et al. 2006. "The JRC-Acquis: A multilingual aligned parallel corpus with 20+ languages." Proceedings of the 5th International Conference on Language Resources and Evaluation (LREC'2006). Genoa, Italy.

Timonera, K. and R. Mitkov. 2015. Improving Translation Memory Matching through Clause Splitting. Proceedings of the RANLP'2015 workshop 'Natural Language Processing for Translation Memories'. Hissar, Bulgaria.

Zhechev, Ventsislav and Josef van Genabith. 2010. Maximising TM Performance through Sub-Tree Alignment and SMT. In *Proceedings of the Ninth Conference of the Association for Machine Translation in the Americas*

Building Dialectal Arabic Corpora

Hani A. Elgabou
Dept. of Computer Science
University of York
York YO10 5DD, UK
he583@york.ac.uk

Dimitar Kazakov
Dept. of Computer Science
University of York
York YO10 5DD, UK
dimitar.kazakov@york.ac.uk

Abstract

The aim of this research is to identify local Arabic dialects in texts from social media (Twitter) and link them to specific geographic areas. Dialect identification is studied as a subset of the task of language identification. The proposed method is based on unsupervised learning using simultaneously lexical and geographic distance. While this study focusses on Libyan dialects, the approach is general, and could produce resources to support human translators and interpreters when dealing with vernaculars rather than standard Arabic.

1 Introduction

The Arabic content on social media is increasingly becoming a mix of modern standard Arabic (MSA) and a collection of different dialects of the Arabic language. It is common to find a degree of this mixture even in Arabic news broadcasts, political dialogues and public events. While almost all mainstream Arabic NLP tools and research focus on MSA, the majority of Arabic dialects are barely touched. With more than 27 spoken varieties of Arabic dialects with a variable degree of intelligibility between them, the need for tools dedicated to dialect processing is essential.

Dialectal corpora would be of an interest to different applications of NLP and information retrieval in general. They would also be useful in building tools and resources, such as dictionaries and terminology databases (Trados, 2017), to aid human translators and interpreters adapt to the local variations of the Arabic language, with partial machine translation and automatic subtitling systems only becoming viable when a substantial body of resources is gathered. Dialect can be used to switch register, and it is not uncommon for Arabic speakers to alternate seamlessly between MSA and their dialects.

All this favours MSA translators and interpreters who have knowledge of the relevant dialects of Arabic, and an automated, large scale effort to provide some of the necessary training resources could play an important role.

The current trend in Arabic NLP regarding the lack of dialectal resources is to try to tackle this problem piecemeal, where researchers build custom tools and methods for a small subset of similar dialects, mainly with the aid of manually crafted datasets. While there is nothing wrong in following such an approach, repeating it for all Arabic dialects is a laborious task.

We believe that there is an alternative that could ease this problem. The proposed approach is based on the use of social media data and carefully crafted clustering and classification methods in order to identify local dialects and link them to geographic areas. The publicly available Twitter messages (also known as *tweets*) offer an opportunity to tag textual data by their geographic location or an approximation of it.

The current research on Arabic dialect classification (which we view as a special case of the task of language identification) only covers a small subset of broadly defined Arabic dialects: Egyptian, Levantine, Iraqi, Jordanian, Tunisian and the one spoken in the Gulf (Zaidan and Callison-Burch, 2014; Huang, 2015; Malmasi et al., 2015). The map in Figure 1 represents a simplified description of the geographic distribution of Arabic dialects, with the actual number of dialects being closer to 25. These, in turn can be further subdivided into variants of each dialect, thus forming a tree. Approaching the problem of dialect classification on a case-by-case basis is a laborious task, and alternatives are needed, as nowadays, language identification is at the heart of many NLP

The Proceedings of the First Workshop on Human-Informed Translation and Interpreting Technology (HiT-IT), pages 52–57,
Varna, Bulgaria, Sept 7, 2017

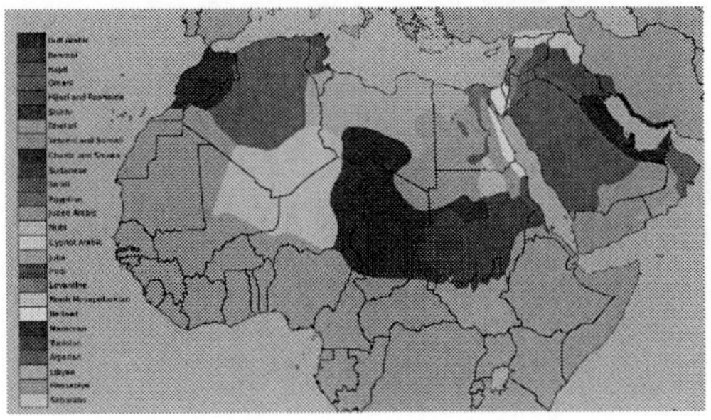

Figure 1: Geographic spread of Arabic dialects (Wikipedia, 2011)

tasks, such as machine translation, question answering and sentiment analysis. The limited capacity for Arabic dialect identification therefore has implications on the ability to carry out NLP for this language, in all its incarnations.

2 Previous Work

Previous work on Arabic dialect identification has mainly used supervised classification methods trained on manually annotated data of n-gram features at both word and character levels (Darwish et al., 2014). Zidan *et al.* (Zaidan and Callison-Burch, 2011, 2014) created a dialect dataset by harvesting reader comments from three local newspapers from three different countries, then used manually annotated data to train a classifier. In the same vein, Bouamor *et al.* (Bouamor et al., 2014) built a multidialectal Arabic parallel corpus of 2,000 sentences cross-translated by native dialect speakers. This dataset includes five dialects in addition to MSA and English.

Diab *et al.* (Diab et al., 2010) started the project COLABA, an effort to create resources and processing tools from dialectal Arabic blogs. COLABA employs human annotators to annotate dialectal words harvested from the blogs in question. The same authors developed DIRA, a term expansion tool for dialectal Arabic. Darwish *et al.* (Darwish et al., 2014) used Morfessor (Creutz and Lagus, 2005), an unsupervised morpheme segmentation tool, to add morphological features to the traditionally used lexical features. Recently, F. Huang from Facebook (Huang, 2015) has adopted a semi-supervised learning approach. Huang trained a classifier on weakly annotated data and another classifier on a small human annotated dataset, then used a combination of both to classify unlabelled data. The reported accuracy gain is 5% compared to previous methods.

Closer to our work is that of Mubarak and Darwish (Mubarak and Darwish, 2014) who show that Twitter can be used to collect dialectal corpora for different Arabic countries using geolocation information associated with Twitter data. They also built a classifier to identify different dialects with accuracy ranging from 95% for the Saudi dialect to 60% for the Algerian. They used a manually extracted list of dialectal n-grams to identify dialectal tweets. Their work is of a special interest for us, as it points out the possible challenges we might face. What differentiates our work is the way in which we collect our data (see below) and our aim to minimise the manual work by using unsupervised learning methods, namely, Expectation Maximisation (Dempster et al., 1977), in addition to supervised learning.

3 Clustering Twitter Data

Twitter data, i.e. tweets and their metadata, present opportunities for various text analysis applications. Tweets are short text messages, with a maximum length of 140 characters, posted by people on the micro-blogging website Twitter. Each tweet comes with its set of metadata fields and values, which contain information such as: the author, creation timestamp, the message, location and more. Table 1 lists some of these fields with their description. Figure 2 presents a detailed view of the data structure of a sample tweet.

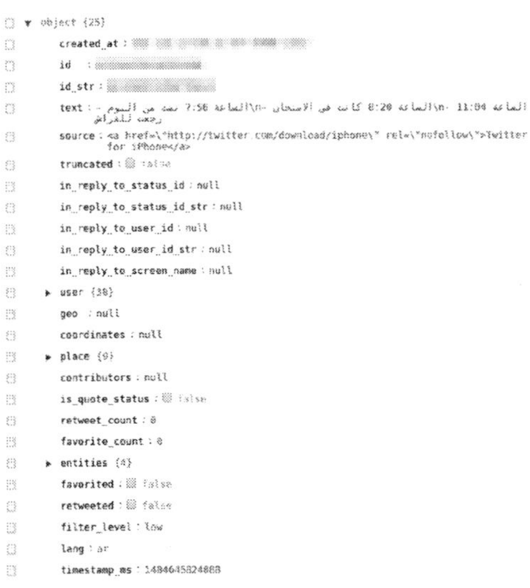

Figure 2: Metadata of a sample tweet

[Field]	Description
[id]	The integer representation of the unique identifier for this Tweet.
[text]	The actual UTF-8 text of the Tweet.
[user]	The user who posted this Tweet.
[coordinates]	The geographic location of this Tweet.
[lang]	language identifier corresponding to the machine-detected language of the Tweet text.
[entities]	Entities mentioned in the text, could be other [user]s, hashtags and/or URLs.

Table 1: Metadata fields of tweets

At this stage we have a particular interest in three fields: $[user]$ to identify dialect speakers, $[text]$ to build our corpora and $[coordinates]$ to identify text by location. We also identified other fields potentially useful if we later chose to use information from social networking between the $[user]$s (Wang et al., 2010) to support our methods.

3.1 Data Collection

Our current primary data collection method is based on filtering the Twitter stream by geographic area. Using Twitter Stream API and its geographic bounding box filter, we are able to collect Tweets from a predefined geographic region. At this point, we are collecting Tweets from the geographic area of Libya as defined by a rectangular bounding box. Figure 3 shows a heatmap distribution of our Tweets data (approx. 700,000 Tweets to date), which is in line with the demographics of the country.

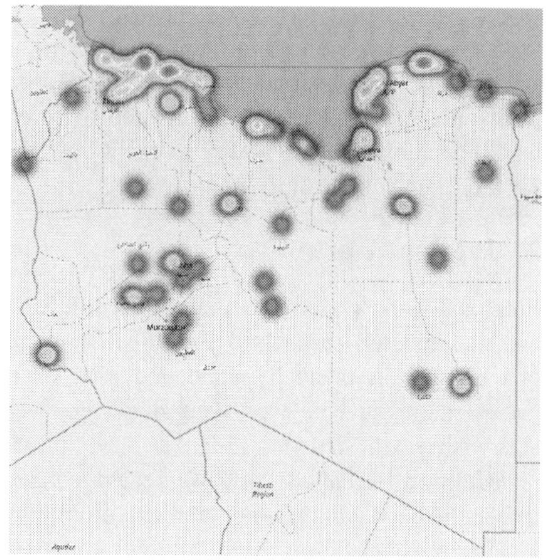

Figure 3: Libyan tweets distribution heatmap

The Twitter API restricts free data collection to just 10% of its actual stream of data. Only paying accounts could get a 100% of the stream, in a package called the Firehose. Since we are using a free account, our data collection is limited to roughly 2700 Tweets a day. Although it would be better to have an access to the Firehose, we managed to overcome some of the limitations of the free data API. The Tweets we are currently collecting on a 24/7 basis are a welcome addition to our dataset, yet our primary aim is to collect as many relevant Twitter accounts as possible. Even one Tweet per account is sufficient. It is easy then to use the Twitter Stream API again to get many more Tweets from each account, with the average around 3000 Tweets per account. (In the future, it is also possible to extend our data by using the Twitter Search API to find Tweets containing already known dialect keywords.)

3.2 Data Preprocessing

As with almost all text from social media, processing Tweets comes with its own set of challenges. Unlike some of the other Internet materials, social media including Tweets show a great variance in text quality. Text could come mixed with non-textual content, URLs, and can contain spelling mistakes and acronyms. Also, the restricted length of the Tweets text limits the amount of information available for text similarity measures (Phan et al., 2008), which are an essential part in most methods and applications of language processing (Hu et al., 2008), be it clustering or classification. The small size also makes it inefficient to represent Tweets using the traditional vector space model.

To tackle the problem of text impurity, we have already implemented python scripts that remove all non-Arabic alphabet text from our data. Since we have no spell checking tools available for the majority of Arabic dialects, we rely on the assumption that the majority of misspelt words would be rare enough to be filtered out by a tf-idf weighting threshold. Since most of our text processing methods are largely dependent on data clustering and classification algorithms, we need an efficient representation of Tweets text that works well with different similarity measures. Although other research has dealt with this problem (Liu et al., 2011; Rosa et al., 2011; Tsur et al., 2013) with different level of efficiency, we decided it will be more natural and convenient for us to cluster the content of entire accounts rather than individual Tweets, as, after all, we are trying to identify different dialect speakers. Therefore, we merge all Tweets from each account into a separate text document and use the results as input to the clustering algorithm. When one user has tweeted from several locations, the most common one is used to provide the geographic coordinates for this account.

3.3 Data Clustering

At this stage we have only run a set of baseline clustering tests to help us understand the problem and the set of challenges we face. To reiterate, we treat the content of each account as a single document, therefore we cluster accounts rather than separate Tweets. This data representation also alows us to overcome the issue of very sparse vector representation of individual Tweets. Each account is represented by an n dimensional vector standing for the words with the n highest scores after the application of tf-idf weighting. Both k-means (MacQueen, 1967) and hierarchical clustering are to be used in order to tune the number of clusters k.

4 Preliminary Results

The results of clustering using geographic distances for $k = 3$ are shown in Figure 5, and appear consistent with the borders of Libyan provinces established since the Antiquity.

Where linguistic distances are concerned, the initial results show some interesting observations. The first observation is that setting the number of clusters k to 3 in k-means gives the most stable clustering results when repeated. The result corresponds well to the above mentioned outcome of spatial clustering, and, in the intuition of the first author, this number reflects well the number of main dialects in Libya. The second observation of note is that for $k = 3$, the centroids of the two largest clusters contain toponyms that represent well the geographic location of these clusters' members through words such as city names and places. This requires careful consideration though as a large number of local toponyms in the data could dominate all text features and create clusters that are naturally correlated with the geographic distribution of Tweets. We still need to establish whether removing the toponyms from the data has a significant effect on the composition of clusters and their spatial distribution.

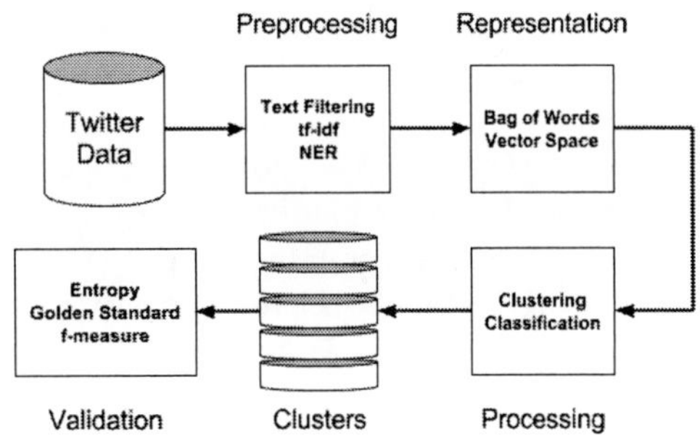

Figure 4: Text processing workflow

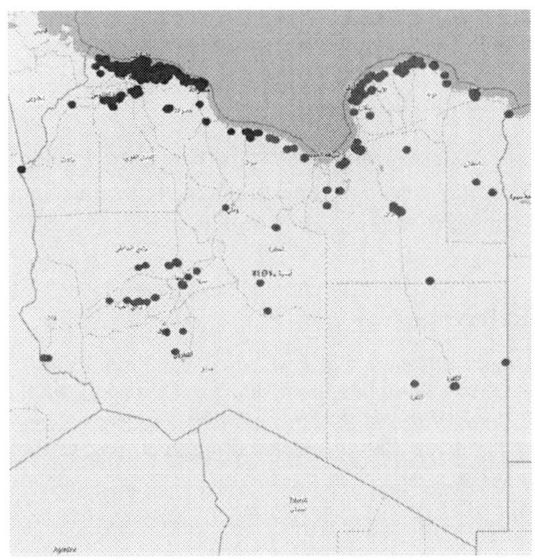

Figure 5: Spatial distance clustering map, $k = 3$

5 Conclusion and Future Work

In our next set of experiments, we are planing to use the Mantel test (Mantel, 1967) in order to measure the correlation between the geographic distances and the lexical distances between pairs of accounts. Clearly, if this correlation was perfect, either set of distances would produce the same clustering. Using the clusters of one set of distances to generate the prior for the other clustering (e.g. using the cluster centroids of spatial clustering to seed k-means for the linguistic clustering step) and vice versa would produce an iterative algorithm that takes into account both metrics, which we are planning to study, along with the effect of different kernels/text features (e.g. word bigrams and part of speech bigrams) on the result. We plan to make our data and dialectal maps available for translators and researchers in general.

Acknowledgments

The authors want to thank the two anonymous reviewers, as well as the workshop chairs and Samy Hedaya for their helpful comments.

References

Houda Bouamor, Nizar Habash, and Kemal Oflazer. 2014. A Multidialectal Parallel Corpus of Arabic. In *the Proc. of the 9th International Conference on Language Resources and Evaluation*. pages 1240–1245.

Mathias Creutz and Krista Lagus. 2005. Unsupervised morpheme segmentation and morphology induction from text corpora using Morfessor 1.0.

Kareem Darwish, Hassan Sajjad, and Hamdy Mubarak. 2014. Verifiably Effective Arabic Dialect Identification. In *the Proc. of the 2014 Conference on Empirical Methods in Natural Language Processing (EMNLP)*. pages 1465–1468.

Arthur P Dempster, Nan M Laird, and Donald B Rubin. 1977. Maximum likelihood from incomplete data via the EM algorithm. *Journal of the Royal Statistical Society. Series B (Methodological)* pages 1–38.

Mona Diab, Nizar Habash, Owen Rambow, Mohamed Altantawy, and Yassine Benajiba. 2010. COLABA: Arabic dialect annotation and processing. In *the Proc. of Lrec workshop on Semitic Language Processing*. pages 66–74.

Jian Hu, Lujun Fang, Yang Cao, Hua-Jun Zeng, Hua Li, Qiang Yang, and Zheng Chen. 2008. Enhancing text clustering by leveraging Wikipedia semantics. In *the Proc. of the 31st Annual International ACM SIGIR Conference on Research and Development in Information Retrieval*. ACM, pages 179–186.

Fei Huang. 2015. Improved Arabic Dialect Classification with Social Media Data. In *the Proc. of the 2015 Conference on Empirical Methods in Natural Language Processing*. pages 2118–2126.

Xiaohua Liu, Kuan Li, Ming Zhou, and Zhongyang Xiong. 2011. Collective semantic role labeling for tweets with clustering. In *the Proc. of the 22nd International Joint Conference on Artificial Intelligence*. volume 3, pages 1832–1837.

James MacQueen. 1967. Some methods for classification and analysis of multivariate observations. In *the Proc. of the 5th Berkeley Symposium on Mathematical Statistics and Probability*. Oakland, CA, USA, pages 281–297.

Shervin Malmasi, Eshrag Refaee, and Mark Dras. 2015. Arabic dialect identification using a parallel multidialectal corpus. In *the Proc. of the International Conference of the Pacific Association for Computational Linguistics*. Springer, pages 35–53.

Nathan Mantel. 1967. The detection of disease clustering and a generalized regression approach. *Cancer Research* 27(2 Part 1):209–220.

Hamdy Mubarak and Kareem Darwish. 2014. Using Twitter to collect a multi-dialectal corpus of Arabic. In *the Proc. of the EMNLP 2014 Workshop on Arabic Natural Language Processing (ANLP)*. pages 1–7.

Xuan-Hieu Phan, Le-Minh Nguyen, and Susumu Horiguchi. 2008. Learning to classify short and sparse text & web with hidden topics from large-scale data collections. In *the Proc. of the 17th International Conference on World Wide Web*. ACM, pages 91–100.

Kevin Dela Rosa, Rushin Shah, Bo Lin, Anatole Gershman, and Robert Frederking. 2011. Topical clustering of tweets. In *Proc. of the ACM SIGIR 3rd Workshop on Social Web Search and Mining (SIGIR–SWSM)*.

SLD Trados. 2017. Terminology Management. [Online; accessed 15-August-2017]. http://www.sdltrados.com/solutions/terminology-management/.

Oren Tsur, Adi Littman, and Ari Rappoport. 2013. Efficient clustering of short messages into general domains. In *the Proc. of the 7th International AAAI Conference on Weblogs and Social Media*.

Xufei Wang, Lei Tang, Huiji Gao, and Huan Liu. 2010. Discovering overlapping groups in social media. In *the Proc. of the 2010 IEEE 10th International Conference - Data Mining(ICDM)*. IEEE, pages 569–578.

Wikipedia. 2011. Varieties of Arabic. [Online; accessed 22-July-2017]. https://en.wikipedia.org/wiki/Varieties_of_Arabic/.

Omar F Zaidan and Chris Callison-Burch. 2011. The Arabic online commentary dataset: An annotated dataset of informal Arabic with high dialectal content. In *the Proc. of the 49th Annual Meeting of the Association for Computational Linguistics: Human Language Technologies: Short Papers-Volume 2*. Association for Computational Linguistics, pages 37–41.

Omar F Zaidan and Chris Callison-Burch. 2014. Arabic dialect identification. *Computational Linguistics* 40(1):171–202.

Towards Producing Human-Validated Translation Resources for the Fula language through WordNet Linking

Khalil Mrini and Martin Benjamin
Ecole Polytechnique Fédérale de Lausanne
Switzerland
{khalil.mrini, martin.benjamin}@epfl.ch

Abstract

We propose methods to link automatically parsed linguistic data to the WordNet. We apply these methods on a trilingual dictionary in Fula, English and French. Dictionary entry parsing is used to collect the linguistic data. Then we connect it to the Open Multilingual WordNet (OMW) through two attempts, and use confidence scores to quantify accuracy. We obtained 11,000 entries in parsing and linked about 58% to the OMW on the first attempt, and an additional 14% in the second one. These links are due to be validated by Fula speakers before being added to the Kamusi Project's database.

1 Introduction

Multilingual dictionaries can be transformed to translation resources through Dictionary Entry Parsing (Lemnitzer and Kunze, 2005; Neff and Boguraev, 1989), that could be used for Machine Translation (Knight and Luk, 1994; Neff and McCord, 1990).

This paper describes first the conversion of a Fula[1] language dictionary (Fulfulde-English-French Lexicon, or FEFL) (Osborn et al., 1993), designed to be read as text, to a structured format that can be interoperable with other languages. The source is a trilingual lexicon offering translations to English and French for each entry. The resulting data is to be added to the Kamusi Project (Benjamin, 1995), which aims to collect linguistic data from many languages, with a special focus on African languages. The Fula language continuum is one of the major members of the Atlantic subfamily of the Niger-Congo languages (Ladefoged, 1968). Varieties, some of which are noted in the source dictionary, are spoken by 24 million people (Parkvall, 2007) in about 21 countries across Western and Central Africa.

To be able to connect Fula to other languages, it must be linked to a lexical base such as the Princeton WordNet (Fellbaum, 1998). Through this, the language is linked to the other languages available in the Open Multilingual WordNet (Bond and Paik, 2012; Bond and Foster, 2013).

This paper proposes a method to link entries collected from a multilingual lexicon to the WordNet. We evaluate each link using a confidence score giving an estimation of its ambiguity. The interoperability with other languages makes this lexicon a language resource that translators and interpreters can use. Finally, this work aims to prepare the collected data for future validation by humans.

2 Parsing

The parsing of a dictionary requires first an analysis of its format. Moreover, both format and content need to be made compatible with Kamusi's own and the data needs to be filtered for relevant categories. In this case, the authors could read the English and French elements of the source dictionary, but had no familiarity with the Fula language. Nor does another data source exist that could shed light on the Fula content due to rare electronic resources. Fortunately, FEFL's lead author provided the lexicon in a machine-readable format.

In this section, we first describe Kamusi's work history and why this resource is emblematic for languishing linguistic data. Then we elaborate on the source dictionary and the parsing method used.

[1] Also known as Fulah, Fulani, Fulfulde, Peul, Pulaar, and Pular. The macrolanguage has ISO 639-3 designation "*ful*", with nine variations assigned individual codes by Ethnologue. `https://www.ethnologue.com/subgroups/fula-1`

The Proceedings of the First Workshop on Human-Informed Translation and Interpreting Technology (HiT-IT), pages 58–64,
Varna, Bulgaria, Sept 7, 2017

```
ABADA Ar
abada, abadaa, abadan DFZ Z<->
never(F) (with negation); ever(F); long ago
jamais(D) (avec la négation)(Z); jamais; il y a longtemps
Abada mi yahaali.  (F): I have never gone.  ; Je ne suis jamais allé.
abada pati (F): don't ever ; ne faîtes jamais (qqch)
gila abada (F): since long ago, forever ; depuis longtemps, toujours
```

Figure 1: Example of an entry in the Fula dictionary

2.1 Kamusi

The goal of Kamusi is to assemble as much linguistic data as possible in a highly structured format under a single umbrella that can be accessed by the public and as linked data for Natural Language Processing (NLP). Within each language, individual senses of each term are considered their own entities. Terms are then joined at the semantic level across languages (with attention to semantic drift and lexical gaps).

The project started with Swahili, and the multilingual expansion was originally planned with a focus on other African languages. As the model was developed and data collection started, though, African languages got pushed toward the rear because no data was available in digital form, or because these languages might have at best a bespoke bilingual electronic or print dictionary with English or French. This resource is therefore a way for Kamusi to strengthen its focus on African languages and address the scarcity of digitally ready African linguistic data.

Even after getting the data and overcoming the challenges for parsing and aligning data, it remains difficult to perform word sense disambiguation automatically (Ide and Véronis, 1998; Lesk, 1986; Navigli, 2009; Rigau and Agirre, 1995). Disambiguation requires human attention, for which the DUCKS (Data Unified Conceptual Knowledge Sets) tool has been developed and is being tested, but it needs resources to develop groups that can work with the lexicons of their languages.

2.2 The Source Dictionary

The source dictionary was begun in 1989. The FEFL authors transmitted the dictionary document for incorporation within Kamusi without copyright restriction. For parsing, the document was converted to plain text.

The FEFL is ordered by the Fula root, with separate entries for each derivative. As a text document, this was a logical way of structuring related Fula terms. However, within our data structure each sense of each word is its own entity, with a feature like "*root*" as one element of the data. Finding all descendants of a common root becomes a function of the search query, rather than a guiding organizational principle.

Each FEFL entry contains at least three lines: first Fula, then English, and finally French. Sometimes, an entry can simply be a cross-reference to the root, performed in one line. That entry might also have lemmas that could be useful for collection. Importantly, as with many multilingual dictionaries, the entries do not contain own-language definitions, but rather ascribe meaning in relation to the given English and French equivalents, and oftentimes Fula usage examples and their translations.

The Fula line begins with at least one Fula lemma and information on the sources, using abbreviations and whether the source ascribes the word to one or more dialects. The Fula language is a continuum with questionable inter-intelligibility from its eastern to western extremes, and it is important to retain the information on dialects as the base for future research. The Fula line also gives abbreviated information on the part-of-speech (PoS) tag. An annex to the dictionary explains all the abbreviations.

The Fula line is followed by the English and then French line, also separated by commas or semicolons. These lines may optionally be followed by annotation lines.

The line for the roots is easily recognizable because the root is written in block capital letters. However, sometimes the line may indicate suffixes to the previous root or a new root. It may also include information on the etymologic origin of the word.

Taking into account the dictionary's specificities is necessary to automatically parse all the entries. An example of an entry is in Figure 1. This example has lemmas in Fula (second line), English (third line) and French (fourth line) with information on sources in parentheses, a line for the root including dialect information (first line) and three lines of annotations at the end.

2.3 Parsing Method

We parsed the source dictionary with a method that evolved as we were able to make sense of the data. It evaluates each non-empty line. We first initiate a new Fula entry. If the current line is not referencing another entry, then there are two cases.

The first case is when the line is a root line. If the Fula entry is complete, meaning it has a root, a Fula line, an English line and a French line, the filtered data is printed into tab-separated text files and a new Fula entry is set. If the line starts with a dash and the current entry's root is non-empty, the suffix is added to that root. Otherwise, the line contains a new root.

The second case is when none of the conditions for the last two have been fulfilled. Then there are two subcases.

The first subcase is when the Fula entry is complete with a root, Fula, English and French lines, then a check is run on the line to see if it is an annotation line that has to be added to the current entry. If the line is instead a line containing at the same time a root and a word, it is ignored. Otherwise, it must be the Fula line of the next entry. Afterwards, the filtered data is first saved and a new Fula entry is initiated with the same root as the previous one and the Fula line is added to it.

The second subcase is when the Fula entry is not complete. If the current line is not an annotation line, it contains either the English or French line, and it is added to the current entry. If the line is found to be an annotation line, the entry is deficient and therefore has to be deleted. We then start looking for a new Fula entry, and this new entry's root is the same as the previous one, unless the next line is a root line.

These two cases ensure all valid Fula entries are collected. However, when valid lines are collected, they are transformed to be cleaned of unnecessary information and separated from information that is considered useful to the preponderance of online dictionary users. The relevant information that is kept is dialects, synonyms that are the lemmas shown in brackets, and PoS tags.

Inside the English and French lines, rough synonyms are separated by commas while different senses are separated by semicolons. The English and French lines both have the same number of synonym sets in the same order, though not necessarily the same number of terms for each concept. The program can thus separate senses into different entries on the base of semicolons, but cannot definitively match specific English terms to specific French terms within synonym sets that can be recognized to share a general topical meaning. For each sense, English information in parentheses is preserved.

At the end, each Fula entry has an ID and inside each entry, each sense has an ID. Eleven tab-separated text files are printed: one for annotations, one for dialects, one for entries that display the Fula line followed by the English and French lines, one for Fula lemmas, one for PoS tags, one for roots, one for sense annotations, one for sense classifications, one for the English sense, one for the French sense and finally one for Fula synonyms. When parsing was completed, the source dictionary resolved to 7918 Fula entries and 10970 Fula senses.

3 Linking to the WordNet

A main purpose of bringing the FEFL data into Kamusi is to make it interoperable with other languages that exploit the same technology. In the case of Fula, this will result in translation resources with neighboring languages such as Songhay and Bambara that have not heretofore been possible. To achieve these objectives, the Fula terms must be connected to the overarching concept sets that Kamusi uses to establish semantic links across languages. Kamusi uses the roughly 100,000 synset definitions from the Princeton WordNet as the starting point for aligning concepts. The nearly 11,000 Fula senses obtained through the parsing procedures described in the previous section can join a larger multilingual database, that is the Open Multilingual WordNet, by being linked to the Princeton WordNet.

3.1 The Princeton WordNet and the Open Multilingual WordNet

The Princeton WordNet (PWN) is an electronic lexical database created in the Cognitive Science Laboratory of Princeton University (Fellbaum, 1998) that separates terms by their senses, and joins terms in "*synsets*" (unordered sets of rough synonyms) that share a general definition. The WordNet concept has now been applied to many other languages, using the PWN synsets as the base set of concepts to populate with the lemmas for their own equivalent terms.

The Open Multilingual WordNet (OMW) (Bond and Foster, 2013) is a collection of standalone wordnets from several dozen languages that could have teams to produce them and have chosen to share their work, with most of their synsets indexed to PWN. If terms from any non-wordnet language can be matched to defined concepts in PWN, they can thus be joined as rough bilingual matches across the OMW.

WordNet divides synsets into four main categories: nouns, verbs, adjectives and adverbs. However, it does not reference function words like prepositions and determiners. So the earlier four parts of speech are the ones that were used to link PWN synsets and the FEFL senses.

3.2 Related Work

Most freely available wordnets use the *expand* method (Vossen, 2005) by adding new lemmas to the existing synsets in the Princeton WordNet. Although Fellbaum and Vossen (2012) argue that this is an imperfect method that poses the question of equivalence, it is useful for this case because FEFL is intended to be understood in reference to the stock of English translation equivalents.

Other wordnets have used the *merge* approach, which Balkova et al. (2004) define as "*building taxonomies from monolingual lexical resources and then, making a mapping process using bilingual dictionaries*". It was used by wordnets such as the Urdu one (Zafar et al., 2012, 2014), whereas the EuroWordNet (Vossen, 1998) is an example of a wordnet using a mixture of both methods. The EuroWordNet also proposed an interlingual index (ILI) (Fellbaum and Vossen, 2008) to tackle concept equivalence between the different languages it contains, whereas Bond et al. (2016) propose a collaborative form of the ILI (CILI) to extend it to all other languages. Kotis et al. (2006) propose an automatic merge approach making use of Latent Semantic Indexing (LSI) (Hofmann, 1999).

3.3 WordNet-linking Method

To understand the method easily, we provide the flowchart in Figure 2 as illustration. Examples of Fula entries will also be used. The Fula word "*adadu*" has the English definition "*quantity, measure; sum, total; calculation; number*". One can notice that senses were separated by a semicolon and synonym terms of the same sense are separated by a comma. In this method, there were two attempts to connect the Fula data through the English translations to the WordNet. The first one considered the senses as separated by semi-colon (step **a** in Figure 2). The second one was more flexible and considered separating senses even further by commas (step **i**). The confidence score formula was adapted to penalize flexibility, as it diminishes accuracy.

In both attempts, the PoS tags were used to identify ID lists of verbs, adjectives and adverbs. Given that 70.4% of senses in the WordNet are nouns, it made sense to have it as the default PoS tag. These lists were used to search for corresponding synsets with the matching PoS tag. For each definition, words were tokenised and stop words were removed unless there was only one word in the definition.

In the first attempt, senses were separated by semicolons. In the above example, 4 senses were obtained. Then, in each sense, the words that were not separated by a comma were joined by an underscore to search for a multiple-word expression in the WordNet (step **b**). For example, the Fula word "*aadamanke*" has the English definition "*human being*". The WordNet was queried for "*human_being*" and gave a set of one synset. However, if this query gave an empty set, then individual words "*human*" and "*being*" would have been matched to the WordNet as in step **c** and a set of synsets is given for each word. Only synsets present in all of the sets were kept (step **d**). This intersection of all non-empty sets became the set of synsets for that sense.

In the instance of the Fula verb "*aatude*", the English definition "*scream loudly, cry out*" has two parts. The first part "*scream loudly*" matches to 3 synsets (step **c**). The second part "*cry out*" matches to 7 synsets (step **b**). They overlap in 1 synset, which will therefore be the only one matching the whole definition (step **d**). Since this final result is determined by more than one non-empty set of synsets, then it is considered the result of an intersection (steps **f** and **h**).

If the final set is an intersection of sets of multiple sub-senses, then there is more confidence in the WordNet matches obtained and so we decided

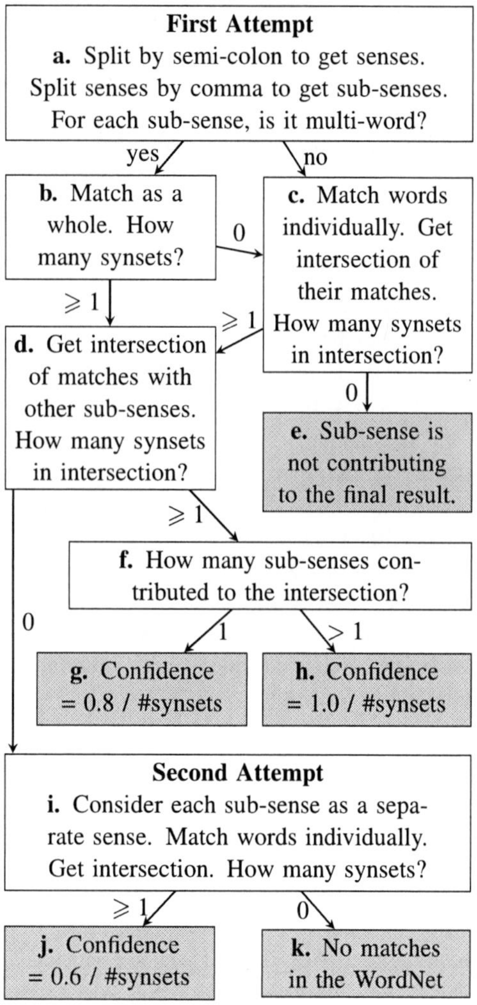

Figure 2: Flowchart of the WordNet-linking method, with final states in gray

to set the confidence score at 1.0 divided by the number of intersecting synsets. If the final set is not an intersection, and therefore was the result of at most a few words not separated by commas, the inaccuracy of not being confirmed multiple times must be penalized. So the confidence score given is 0.8 divided by the number of synsets in the final set (step **g**).

In the second attempt (step **i**), the Fula entries considered are those left unconnected to the WordNet in the prior attempt. The words in the senses, here defined by separation both by commas and semicolons, are not joined by an underscore for WordNet matching but are rather matched individually. So the final set will be the intersection of these words' synset matches. For instance, the Fula verb "*aalude*" has English definition "*split, dissociate*". This sense has two parts when we split by comma. No common synset could be found between the two parts. Therefore, we split the sense by comma and obtained two senses "*split*" and "*dissociate*". These have separate matches in the WordNet and therefore the confidence score is also separate.

This second attempt is more flexible than the first one. So for each sense it matched, the confidence score will be 0.6 divided by the number of synsets in the final set (step **j**). The confidence scores were computed such that the greater the ambiguity, the lower the score. Items that have only one match to the WordNet can be clearly distinguished, as their scores will be either 1, 0.8 or 0.6. Meanwhile, items that have multiple WordNet matches (0.5 or below) are quickly filtered out to diminish ambiguity. In the end, the confidence scores proved useful in determining whether an entry could be accepted as-is, or placed in Kamusi's DUCKS tool for human review.

3.4 Results and Discussion

The links automatically established by the WordNet-linking method are in Table 1. 72.4% of all Fula senses were linked to the WordNet. Links with confidence score 1.0 indicate an almost-certain match, whereas links with confidence score 0.8 or 0.6 indicate likely matches. At the end, 3031 Fula senses (27.6% of total) remained without any potential WordNet connections.

Such examples of Fula words that ended up without WordNet connections include pronouns (such as "*you*") that the WordNet does not include. Because some non-noun words were not PoS-tagged in the FEFL and because of the assumption that all entries without PoS tags were nouns, non-PoS-tagged entries such as "*never*" and "*ever*" that are adverbs could not be matched. In other cases, matches were not found between concepts because the sources use different terms to render a similar idea, such as "*person who is knowledgeable*" in the FEFL versus "*wise man*" in PWN. Still other non-matches are due to different patterns for expressing concepts that have a shared cultural existence, such as the verb "*seyadde*", that in English is "*be*" plus the adjective "*happy*".

However, a large (uncounted) number of unmatched Fula words are very specific to the Central and Western African context. Such words are

Attempt	Initial senses	Senses linked	**Confidence score**: Senses with 1 link
First	10970	58.3% (6391)	**1.0:** 5.2% (332); **0.8:** 20.3% (1295)
Second	4579	3543 sub-definitions linked, which resulted from 1548 senses (14.1%)	**0.6:** 16.4% (581)

Table 1: Results of the two WordNet-linking attempts as applied on the FEFL senses

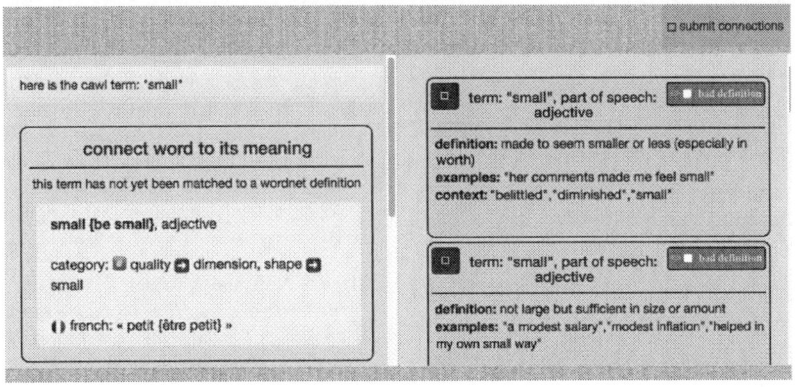

Figure 3: Live version of DUCKS, with the Comparative African Word List (CAWL) as active dataset

for instance the verb "*furraade*" which has the English translation "*break the fast at sunset*", or the noun "*maari*" which means in English "*condiment made from seeds of the locust bean tree*". From the perspective of Digital Humanities, these words that do not have a linguistic or conceptual equivalent in English are perhaps the most interesting result of mining a dictionary that grew from field lexicography, revealing indigenous concepts and making them visible to the global knowledge base.

3.5 Future Work

Subsequent steps include: making the data searchable online with its original trilingual sets and validating the data by humans through DUCKS.

DUCKS has been developed so that players are presented with a term in their native language on one side of their screen, and a list of WordNet senses for the given English equivalent. Then, players can chose which senses match the term, as in Figure 3. This crowd-sourced validation can replace the one performed by authors of wordnets such as the Japanese (Isahara et al., 2008) and Arabic (Black et al., 2006) ones. The success rate of our algorithm will be determined by the number of WordNet links approved by Fula speakers.

The senses with no match to the WordNet are ineligible for DUCKS until further human review, that might establish other existing English terms for alignment.

4 Conclusions

This paper proposed methods to collect linguistic data automatically using dictionary entry parsing and wordnet linking. We applied these methods to a trilingual Fula-English-French lexicon (FEFL) (Osborn et al., 1993).

First, a thorough analysis of the format of the dictionary was necessary in order to parse it and collect the necessary data, with the method being refined empirically. At the end, the parsing resulted in 7918 Fula entries and 10970 Fula senses gathered, organised in 11 categories of useful data.

Then, to provide a base for semantic comparison, the Fula data was linked to the Princeton WordNet (Fellbaum, 1998). Through this linking, it is connected to all languages available in the Open Multilingual WordNet (Bond and Foster, 2013). Two attempts were made, with the second one being more flexible. Confidence scores were given to each match, to gauge their accuracy. The first attempt scored 6391 potential matches whereas the second one scored 3543 matches. In total, 72.4% of the Fula senses were linked. Many of the 3031 unmatched Fula senses were related to the specific cultural and geographical context where the language is used.

This automatically collected and linked translation resource will be put in DUCKS to be validated by Fula speakers, before joining Kamusi data.

References

Valentina Balkova, Andrey Sukhonogov, and Sergey Yablonsky. 2004. Russian wordnet. In *Proceedings of the Second Global Wordnet Conference*.

Martin Benjamin. 1995. Kamusi gold (global online living dictionary). Accessed: 2017-08-04. https://kamusi.org/.

William Black, Sabri Elkateb, Horacio Rodriguez, Musa Alkhalifa, Piek Vossen, Adam Pease, and Christiane Fellbaum. 2006. Introducing the arabic wordnet project. In *Proceedings of the third international WordNet conference*. pages 295–300.

Francis Bond and Ryan Foster. 2013. Linking and extending an open multilingual wordnet. In *ACL (1)*. pages 1352–1362.

Francis Bond and Kyonghee Paik. 2012. A survey of wordnets and their licenses. *Small* 8(4):5.

Francis Bond, Piek Vossen, John P McCrae, and Christiane Fellbaum. 2016. Cili: the collaborative interlingual index. In *Proceedings of the Global WordNet Conference*. volume 2016.

Christiane Fellbaum. 1998. *WordNet*. Wiley Online Library.

Christiane Fellbaum and Piek Vossen. 2008. Challenges for a global wordnet. In *Online Proceedings of the First International Workshop on Global Interoperability for Language Resources*. pages 75–82.

Christiane Fellbaum and Piek Vossen. 2012. Challenges for a multilingual wordnet. *Language Resources and Evaluation* 46(2):313–326.

Thomas Hofmann. 1999. Probabilistic latent semantic indexing. In *Proceedings of the 22nd annual international ACM SIGIR conference on Research and development in information retrieval*. ACM, pages 50–57.

Nancy Ide and Jean Véronis. 1998. Introduction to the special issue on word sense disambiguation: the state of the art. *Computational linguistics* 24(1):2–40.

Hitoshi Isahara, Francis Bond, Kiyotaka Uchimoto, Masao Utiyama, and Kyoko Kanzaki. 2008. Development of the japanese wordnet. .

Kevin Knight and Steve K Luk. 1994. Building a large-scale knowledge base for machine translation. In *AAAI*. volume 94, pages 773–778.

Konstantinos Kotis, George A Vouros, and Konstantinos Stergiou. 2006. Towards automatic merging of domain ontologies: The hcone-merge approach. *Web semantics: Science, services and agents on the world wide web* 4(1):60–79.

Peter Ladefoged. 1968. *A phonetic study of West African languages: An auditory-instrumental survey*. 1. Cambridge University Press.

Lothar Lemnitzer and Claudia Kunze. 2005. Dictionary entry parsing. *ESSLLI-2005* .

Michael Lesk. 1986. Automatic sense disambiguation using machine readable dictionaries: how to tell a pine cone from an ice cream cone. In *Proceedings of the 5th annual international conference on Systems documentation*. ACM, pages 24–26.

Roberto Navigli. 2009. Word sense disambiguation: A survey. *ACM Computing Surveys (CSUR)* 41(2):10.

Mary S Neff and Branimir K Boguraev. 1989. Dictionaries, dictionary grammars and dictionary entry parsing. In *Proceedings of the 27th annual meeting on Association for Computational Linguistics*. Association for Computational Linguistics, pages 91–101.

Mary S Neff and Michael C McCord. 1990. *Acquiring lexical data from machine-readable dictionary resources for machine translation*. IBM Thomas J. Watson Research Division.

Donald W. Osborn, David J. Dwyer, and Joseph I. Donohoe Jr. 1993. *A Fulfulde (Maasina)-English-French Lexicon: A Root-based Compilation Drawn from Extant Sources Followed by English-Fulfulde and French-Fulfulde Listings*. Michigan State University Press.

Mikael Parkvall. 2007. Världens 100 största språk 2007. *The World's* 100.

German Rigau and Eneko Agirre. 1995. Disambiguating bilingual nominal entries against wordnet. *arXiv preprint cmp-lg/9510004* .

Piek Vossen. 1998. Introduction to eurowordnet. *Computers and the Humanities* 32(2-3):73–89.

Piek Vossen. 2005. Building wordnets. Accessed: 2017-08-07. http://www.globalwordnet.org/gwa/BuildingWordnets.ppt.

Ayesha Zafar, Afia Mahmood, Farhat Abdullah, Saira Zahid, Sarmad Hussain, and Asad Mustafa. 2012. Developing urdu wordnet using the merge approach. In *Proceedings of the Conference on Language and Technology*. pages 55–59.

Ayesha Zafar, Afia Mahmood, Sana Shams, and Sarmad Hussain. 2014. Structural analysis of linking urdu wordnet to pwn 2.1. In *the Proceedings of Conference on Language and Technology 2014 (CLT14)*.